THE COMIC TOOLBOX

HOW TO BE FUNNY EVEN IF YOU'RE NOT

BY JOHN VORHAUS

SILMAN-JAMES PRESS
Los Angeles

First Edition

20   19   18   17   16   15   14   13   12   11

Library of Congress Cataloging-in-Publication Data

Vorhaus, John
The comic toolbox : how to be funny ever if you're not /
by John Vorhaus
p. cm.
1. Comic, The. 2. Comedy--Technique. I. Title
PN1922.V59   1994   808.7--dc20   94-33037

ISBN: 1-879505-21-5

Cover Design by Heidi Frieder

Printed and bound in the United States of America

Silman-James Press
1181 Angelo Drive
Beverly Hills, CA 90210

TO MAXX, WHO SAYS I MAKE HER LAUGH

CONTENTS

ACKNOWLEDGEMENTS

If I thanked everybody there was to thank, the acknowledgements would run longer than the book. So thanks to Al and Louise, Nancy and Jim, who may have wondered but never doubted. Thanks to Bill for keeping me on the path and Scott for not letting me off the hook. Thanks to Cliff, who was there at the birth of the *Toolbox*. Thanks also to Linda and Barbara at the UCLA Extension Writer's Program. Finally I'd like to thank all my students, from whom I've learned so much.

"FORWARD!"
to *The Comic Toolbox*

Are you one of those sorry folk
Who cannot write a decent joke,
Who cannot pen a funny scene
Because you lack the comic gene?
Are you convinced that you alone
Are cursed to walk this earth without a funny bone?
Take heart, dear friend, for now a book is writ
To guide you on your quest
To wrest from deep within, your native wit.
Voilà! *The Comic Toolbox* by John Vorhaus
To save you from the jester's poorhouse.
It lays you certain basic rules
That aid the craft of serious fools.
You'll learn to slay that dreaded djin,
The Editor who lives within.
And once sprung from that self-constructed jail,
You'll then be free to risk and free to fail.
Free to find the premise, choose the word
That separates the master from the nerd.
So if you wish to tune your comic craft
And join the ranks of the professionally daft,
Then take this book of humor-honing tools
And join the ranks of jesters, clowns and fools
Who rise each day and, taking out their pen,
Bring joy and laughter to their fellow men.

—Peter Bergman,
Firesign Theatre, Los Angeles, 1994

INTRODUCTION

There's a book by William Strunk and E.B. White called *The Elements of Style*. When we read it in high school, my friends and I all called it *The Elephants of Style*, and you can be sure that we thought that this was pretty much the height of hilarity. Well, we also thought that drinking a great deal of Boone's Farm apple wine and throwing up on neighbors' lawns was a good idea, so draw your own conclusions. At any rate, *The Elements of Style* was a seminal book—it packed a ton of useful information about language and writing (and even, in its own offhand way, about life) into a very small number of pages. For a grammar text, it was, and remains, a remarkably good read. I recommend it.

Strunk and White were big on rules and not at all afraid to take a stand. They hated the passive voice, for instance, and insisted that use of the passive voice led to weak writing. Because I was young and impressionable when I read their book, I made this rule my own. For most of my writing life, I religiously purged the passive voice from my work.

And then one day I discovered how much fun it was to write in the passive voice. I knew it was wrong; Bill and E.B. had told me it was wrong. But I couldn't help myself. The words just came spilling out onto the page:

> *The room was walked into by a man by whom strong, handsome features were had. A woman was met by him. The bed was lain upon by her. Then the bed was lain upon by him. Clothing was removed from them both. Sex was had. Climax was achieved. Afterward, cigarettes were smoked*

by them. Suddenly, the door was opened by the husband of the woman by whom the bed was lain upon. A gun was held by him. Some screams were screamed and angry words exchanged. Jealousy was felt by the man by whom the gun was held. Firing of the gun was done by him. The flying of bullets took place. Impact was felt by bodies. The floor was hit by bodies. Remorse was then felt by the man by whom the gun was held. The gun was turned upon himself.

And the rest, as they say, is forensics.

So slavish had I been in my devotion to the so-called rules of good writing that I had missed out on a piece of real linguistic merriment—a joke, if nothing else. In blind obeisance to the rules, I forgot to have fun. And jeez, if you can't have fun in writing, or painting or drawing, or acting or twisting balloon animals, or indeed any creative endeavor, why bother?

So I want to make one thing clear going in: The first rule is that there are no rules. Take *all* this stuff with a huge, crystalline grain of salt. My tools are my tools, designed for my convenience. If you find them useful, by all means use them. But they're not gospel, for God's sake, nor even elements of style.

On the other hand, I believe very strongly that the rules don't confine, they define. Creativity is problem-solving. The more (useful) rules we have, and the more rigorously we apply them, the more clearly we understand the problem we're trying to solve, and the more success we'll have at solving it. For instance, if your car has a dead battery, it's a rule that you connect the jumper cables plus-to-plus and minus-to-ground. Connect the plus terminal of one battery to the minus terminal of the other and you'll end up with a fried battery, and possibly a fried face.

So as you poke around in this thing called *The Comic Toolbox,* adopt the useful fiction that everything in it is at least worthy of consideration. If you test these tools and find them user unfriendly, by all means reject them. In doing so, you'll likely come up with some new ones of your own. They'll be better for you, because they'll be yours, conceived by you in an idiom that you understand. But do try out all the tools.

And especially try the exercises.

Some may seem difficult, or irrelevant to your work, or just plain stupid. Try them anyhow, if only to prove how just plain stupid they really are. As I'll take pains to make clear later on, you won't be graded on your work, nor judged in any sense—not even by you. But you will get much more out of all this material if you put it into play while it's all fresh in your mind. Scrawl in the margins if you like, or write down your answers in self-deleting computer files if that will help you minimize your emotional risk. But do try the exercises. You'll only get out of this book what you put in. Or to put it another way, the more you pay, the more it's worth.

Several years ago, I taught a class called Writing from the Alien Perspective. As homework for that class, I assigned the following: "Go out and do something new, something you've never done before." Some people paid for strangers' meals. Some stole library books. Some played dumb. Some refused to do the assignment, which is something they'd never done before in any class anywhere. Some got arrested. It was that sort of exercise.

And we discovered something very interesting. The mere act of doing the unexpected thing created one funny moment after another. That revelation led to a new class, called The Comic Toolbox, and that class led to this book. So as you read the book, stop frequently to ask yourself how you can make your creative process fresh and new. I'm not talking about what you write or draw or paint, but about the system by which you bring your material to life. Break old habits, even ones that work. Write in bed. Paint in the park. Draw cartoons on walls. Take yourself by surprise; the more you do this, the funnier you'll be. If nothing else, you'll have the experience of doing something new, and the new thing is almost always worth doing, if for nothing but the newness alone.

A blanket disclaimer before we push on: in this book, I talk a lot about the hero and the character and the writer and reader and viewer. A lot of times I call these people he, though of course I mean both he and she. Language lags behind social change, and the English language still lacks an easy convention for gender-neutral third-person pronouns. Maybe Strunk and White could sort it out, but I've just had to muddle through. Thanks for bearing with me.

Eastern philosophy describes creativity as "carrying buckets to the river." The river is always there, but sometimes the buckets don't do their job. As much as anything else, this is a book about building better buckets. Some of them work well for me, and I hope they work well for you, too.

Sydney, Australia
April, 1994

1
COMEDY IS TRUTH AND PAIN

When I was twelve years old, I fell in love with Leslie Parker. She was cute and smart, with blond hair in bangs, and a smile that made my head sweat. All through seventh grade, through lunch hours and band practice and the first yearning boy-girl parties of my aggrieved adolescence, I mooned after that girl as only a hormonally enraged lunatic in the throes of puppy love can moon. I was a sad case.

And then, one day during math class, while thirty sweaty youngsters in bellbottom pants and "Let It All Hang Out" T-shirts pondered the imponderables of pi, Leslie Parker mentioned in passing that she and her family were moving away. My world imploded like a dark star. The amputation of a cherished body part could not have hurt me worse. My hand shot into the air.

The teacher, Mr. Desjardins, ignored me. He did that a lot because, I think, I was always asking vexing questions like, "What's the square root of minus one?" and "*Why* can't you divide by zero?" I waved my hand like an idiot, trying to get his attention. No go.

Ten minutes pass, and Leslie Parker's stunning revelation fades from everybody's mind but mine. At last, just before the bell, Mr. Desjardins casts a reluctant nod my way. I stand up. Pathetically and wildly inappropriately, I bleat, "Leslie, *where* are you moving, and *why*?" By which, of course, I mean, "Don't *leave* me!"

There was sudden stunned silence, for I had committed the cardinal sin of seventh grade. In a classic act of bad timing, I had revealed my feelings. In the next instant, everyone burst out laughing. Even Mr. Desjardins, that sadist, smothered a chortle in a shirt cuff. Let me tell you that the instant is etched in my memory like acid on a photographic plate, the single most painful and humiliating moment of my life up to that point. (The last such moment? Oh, would that it were so. Remind me some day to tell you about the college co-ed shower fiasco.) And I'll never forget what Mr. Desjardins said as my classmates' laughter rang in my ears, and Leslie Parker looked at me like road kill. "They're not laughing at you, Mr. Vorhaus. They're laughing *with* you."

He was lying, of course. They were laughing at me. All those little monsters were just taking ghoulish delight in my shame. And why? Because they knew, in their tiny, insecure, prepubescent hearts, that, though I was the one who had stepped on the land mine that time, it could have been any one of them. And so in one single heartbreaking and mortifying instant, I discovered a fundamental rule of humor, though it was many years (and many, many years of therapy) before I recognized it as such:

COMEDY IS TRUTH AND PAIN.

I'll repeat it for you bookstore browsers who are just grazing here to see if this tome is your cup of cranial tea: *Comedy is truth and pain.*

When I debased myself before Leslie Parker, I experienced the truth of love and the pain of love lost.

When a clown catches a pie in the face, it's truth and pain. You feel for the poor clown all covered with custard, and you also realize that it could have been you, sort of *there but for the grace of pie go I.*

Traveling-salesman jokes are truth and pain. The truth is that the salesman wants something, and the pain is that he's never going to get it. In fact, almost every dirty joke rests on truth and pain, because sex is a harrowing experience that we all share—with the possible exception of one Willard McGarvey, who was even more pathetic than I was in seventh grade, and who grew up to become a Benedictine monk. I wonder if Willard's reading this book. Hello, Willard.

The truth is that relations between the sexes are problematic. The pain is that we have to deal with the problems if we want the rewards. Consider the following joke:

> *Adam says to God, "God, why did you make*

women so soft?" God says, "So that you will like them." Adam says, "God, why did you make women so warm and cuddly?" God says, "So that you will like them." Adam says to God, "But, God, why did you make them so stupid?" God says, "So that they will like you."

The joke takes equal shots at the attitudes both of men and women. It makes men look bad, it makes women look bad, but behind all that, there's shared common experience: We're all human, we all have gender, and we're all in this ridiculous soup together. That's truth, that's pain, and that's what makes a joke jump.

In a classic episode of *I Love Lucy*, Lucille Ball gets a job in a candy factory where the conveyor belt suddenly starts going faster and faster, leaving poor Lucy desperately stuffing candy in her mouth, trying to stay ahead of the belt. What's the truth? That situations can get out of hand. And the pain? We pay for our failures.

Even greeting cards boil down to truth and pain. "I'll bet you think this envelope is too small for a present," says the cover of the card. And inside? "Well, you're right." That's truth *(I'm cheap)*, and that's pain *(so you lose)*.

My grandfather used to tell this joke:

A bunch of men are standing outside the pearly gates, waiting to get into heaven. St. Peter approaches and says, "All you men who were henpecked by your wives during your lives, go to the left wall. All you men who weren't henpecked, go to the right wall." All the men go to the left wall except one timid little old man, who goes to the right wall. St. Peter crosses to the little old man and says, "All these other men were henpecked in their lives; they went to the left wall. How come you went to the right wall?" Says the little old man, "My wife told me to."

Truth and pain. The truth is that some men, sometimes, are henpecked, and the pain is that some men, sometimes, are stuck with it.

There's something else present in this joke, and that's fear of death. Now, some philosophers argue that all human experience reduces to fear of death, so even buying a cheap card instead of a birthday present somehow relates to mortality. Maybe. I dunno. This book is not concerned with such ponderous possibilities. If it were, it would be called *The Philosophical Toolbox: How to be Heavy, Even if You're Not.* Nevertheless, it's true that death, like sex, is fundamental to the human experience. Is it any wonder, then, that so many of our jokes turn on the truth and pain of death?

> *A man dies and goes to hell. Satan tells him that he'll be shown three rooms, and whichever room he chooses will be his home for all eternity. In the first room, thousands of people are screaming in the agony of endless burning flame. The man asks to see the second room. In the second room, thousands of people are being rent limb from limb by horrible instruments of torture. The man asks to see the third room. In the third room, thousands of people are standing around drinking coffee while raw sewage laps around their knees. "I'll take this room," says the man. Whereupon Satan yells out to the crowd, "Okay, coffee break's over! Everybody back on your head!"*

The truth? There might be a hell. And the pain? It might be hell.

> *A man falls off a cliff. As he plummets, he's heard to mutter, "So far, so good."*

The truth and the pain: Sometimes we're victims of fate.

Religion is similarly an experience that touches us all, because it tries so hard to explain those other human fundamentals, sex and death. Jokes that poke fun at religious figures and situations do so by exposing the truth and the pain of the religious experience: We want to believe; we're just not sure we do.

What do you get when you cross a Jehovah's Witness with an agnostic?
Someone who rings your doorbell for no apparent reason.

The truth is that some people strive for faith. The pain is that not everybody gets there. And by the way, people who don't "get" a joke, or take offense at it, often feel that way because they don't accept the "truth" that the joke presents. A Jehovah's Witness wouldn't find this joke funny because he *has* faith, and thus doesn't buy the so-called truth that the joke tries to sell.

Look, it's not my intention to prove or disprove the existence of God or the value of faith. My beliefs, your beliefs don't enter into it. What makes a thing funny is how it impacts the *generally held beliefs* of the audience hearing the joke. Religion and sex and death are rich areas for humor because they touch some pretty strongly held beliefs.

But it doesn't have to be that way. You can also find truth and pain in small events: *Why does the dieting man never get around to changing a light bulb? Because he's always going to start tomorrow.* The truth is that the human will has limits, and the pain is that we can't always transcend those limits. If you want to know why a thing is funny, ask yourself what truth and what pain does that thing express.

Take a moment now and tell yourself a few of your favorite jokes. Ask yourself what truth and what pain is suggested in each joke. Consider that this truth and this pain are the theme of the joke.

As you'll notice, not all themes are universal. After all, not everyone is on a diet, or henpecked, or even afraid to die, though most of us know someone who is on a diet, henpecked, afraid of death, or all of the above. Humor works on the broad sweep of big truth and big pain, but it also works on the intimate level of small truth and small pain. The trick is to make sure that your audience has the same points of reference as you.

When a stand-up comic makes a joke about bad airplane food, he's mining a common vein of truth and pain. Everyone can relate. Even if you've never flown, you know airplane food's, shall we say, ptomainic reputation. You get the joke.

You don't have to be a stand-up comic, or even a comic writer, to use the tool of truth and pain. If you were giving an after-dinner speech, for example, you could start your talk with something that acknowledges the truth and the pain of the situation.

> *"I know you're all anxious to get up and stretch after that long meal, so I'll try to be brief." (Pause.)*
> *"Thank you and good night."*

The truth is that speeches run long, and the pain is that audiences get bored. The savvy speechmaker cops to this reality. For reasons we'll discuss later, you often don't have to tell a joke to get a laugh; sometimes you just have to tell the truth.

Sadly, politically incorrect humor, like sexist or racist jokes, also trades on truth and pain. Let's see if I can show you what I mean without offending anyone.

Suppose there's a group called the Eastsiders and a rival group called the Westsiders, and these two groups tell jokes about each other. From an Eastsider, then, you might hear a line like, "If a Westside couple divorces, are they still cousins?"

The Eastsiders, as a group, hold in common the truth that Westsiders are venal or immoral or stupid. Their common pain is that *we* have to put up with *them*. I won't press this point, since I have no desire to teach racists or sexists how better to practice their craft. Suffice it to say that any human experience, no matter how large or how small, can be made to be funny if its truth and and its pain are readily identifiable to the target audience.

In television situation comedies, for example, you'll hear more jokes about body parts than about sacred texts, because most viewers (and I'm willing to bet on this) know more about butt cracks than the *Bhagavad-Gita*.

Here's a joke that a lot of people don't get:

> *"How many solipsists does it take to screw in a light bulb?"*
> *"Who wants to know?"*

This joke is only funny (and then only barely) if you know that a solipsist believes in nothing but his own existence (and in that only barely), and so is forever and always alone in his world. When you throw a joke like this at an unsuspecting audience, you make them work far too hard to discover its truth and pain. By the time they sort it all out, if indeed they do, the moment has passed and the joke is no longer funny.

The difference between a class clown and a class nerd is that the class clown tells jokes everyone gets while the class nerd tells jokes that only he gets. Comedy, thus, is not just truth and pain, but universal, or at least general, truth and pain.

But wait, there's more. We know from the commutative property of addition that if comedy = truth + pain, then truth + pain = comedy as well. (See? I learned something else in seventh grade math beyond the fact that love makes you stupid.) So if you're dying to be funny even if you're not, simply pick a situation and seek to sum up its truth and pain.

Any situation will work. A trip to the dentist. A family vacation. Getting money from an ATM. Doing your taxes. Reading this book. Cramming for an exam. Anything. Anything. Because every situation has at least some implied truth and pain. Suppose you're studying for a big test. The truth is, it's important to pass. The pain is, you're not prepared. The joke that encompasses this truth and pain (using the tool of exaggeration, which we'll discuss later) might be:

> *I'm such a lousy student, I couldn't pass a blood test.*

See how easy?

Okay, okay, I know it's not that easy. After all, if everything you needed to know about comedy were right here in chapter one, then you could read this whole book standing in the checkout line, and I'd be out a not inconsiderable royalty.

Also, let's not kid ourselves. This book won't make you funny, not by itself. That'll only happen if you do a lot of hard work along the way. And it won't happen overnight. No reason why it should. Look at it this way: Suppose you wanted to be a wood carver, and someone told you there was a thing called an adze, great for carving wood. "Wow," you'd say, "an adze! Imagine that." Just knowing that the thing exists, of course, gives you no clue how to use it, and further, knowing how to use it doesn't mean you're going to carve a teak *Pietà* on the first try. You have to learn to crawl, to coin a phrase, before you can pitch forward on your face.

2
THE WILL TO RISK

A newspaper reporter called me not long ago. Since I'm now some sort of soi-disant expert on the subject of comedy, this reporter wanted to know if I thought that there were people with absolutely *no* sense of humor. Was it possible, the writer wondered, to be completely and irremediably unfunny?

The question put me in mind of my first boss, a moon-faced woman with a Hitlerian haircut who cherished the notion that junior advertising copywriters should be seen and not heard. One day, in a fit of nihilistic spunk, I put a live goldfish in her tea. Soon I was collecting unemployment. "No sense of humor," I thought at the time, but I now see that all she lacked was *my* sense of humor. The fact is, not everyone agrees on what's funny.

But everyone *can* be funny, and that's what I told the reporter. If people aren't funny, there are usually two things lacking. One is an understanding of what's funny and why, which we'll tackle in due time. The other, far more important, element is the *will to risk*. To my mind, the will to risk is a tool, and like other tools, it can be learned and understood and mastered.

Yes, yes, yes, some people have more natural humor in them than others, just like some people have perfect pitch or a knack for hitting the curve ball. Most of us have more humor than we know. What we don't always have is the will to risk, and the will to risk is really the will to fail. We're taught from early youth to abhor failure, but odd as it may seem, a willingness to fail is one of the most valuable tools in your comic toolbox. It makes all of your other tools easier to use, and use well.

So the first big task of this toolbox is to boost our will to risk.

And the first step in that direction is to . . .

ERADICATE BOGUS THINKING

Of course, there's all sorts of bogus thinking in this world: aerosol cheese is a good idea; just one cigarette's okay; the little red light on the dashboard doesn't *really* mean anything's wrong. I now commend to your attention two particularly insidious types of bogus thinking: *false assumptions* and *faulty associations.*

When we think about telling a joke, or trying a new idea, or, really, engaging in any creative act, there lurks behind our conscious thinking the following false assumption: *It won't work; they won't like it.* So in the moment between thinking a joke and telling a joke, the "unfunny" person throws this huge roadblock in his or her own way. It won't work. They won't like it. Maybe I'll just keep my big yap shut, play it safe; yeah, that's the thing to do. And that's just what they usually do. And so we think of them as shy or repressed or boring. A drag, and no fun at parties.

Okay, so why is *it won't work* a false assumption? After all, maybe it *won't* work. Maybe they won't like it. Well, true, that's a possibility. But we have a whole body of hard evidence to the contrary. Sometimes jokes *do* work, so the assumption of failure is inherently at least partly wrong. Every bit as wrong, that is, as the assumption of success. You just won't know until you try.

So why not try? What have we got to lose? In fact, deep in our secret hearts, we feel—or fear—that we have a *great deal* to lose. That's where the *faulty association* comes in. Having first decided, most bogusly, that our joke won't work, we leap to the amazing conclusion that when "they" don't like our joke, "they" won't like *us* either. We create within our minds the grim certainty that we will look stupid or foolish or otherwise diminished in someone else's eyes. Why is this a faulty association? For this simple reason: People aren't thinking about how you look to them. They're far too busy worrying how *they* look to you.

Each of us is the center of our own universe, and our universe is of surprisingly little interest to the universe next door. Burdened by our fears, we jump through hoops to keep from looking bad in others' eyes. But as it says in the *Koran,* if you knew how little people thought about you, you wouldn't worry what they thought.

And then, just to thicken the glue, we throw in one more faulty association: "When they don't like me, I can't like myself." Man, this one's scary. We spend so much time fortifying our self-image with what others think that by the time we get around to firing off a joke, our entire ego is on the line. If the joke misfires, ego-death must result. That's why a stand-up comic says, "I died out there" when a show goes bad. Behind all the bogus thinking is the biggest bogus thought of all: If I fail, I die.

Let's look at the whole loop again, just to make sure we understand it. You open your mouth to tell a joke, but a little voice says, "Hang on, that might not work." Then another little voice answers, "Of course it won't work, and when it doesn't work, you'll look like a failure, a fool." And a third voice chimes in, "If you're a fool to them, you're a fool to you, too." And finally, "Your ego will die; then *you* will die." That's a big burden for one poor little joke to carry, is it not?

Look, I can't straighten out all these self-image issues in one slim chapter in a book that's not even about that anyhow. If I could, the book would be called *The Ego Toolbox: How to be Totally Together and Really Well-Adjusted, Even if You're Not.* But what I can do is give you some strategies and tactics for silencing those bogus voices in your head. Here's the first, and most valuable:

KILL YOUR FEROCIOUS EDITOR

Gather all your bogus voices, tie them together in a metaphorical knot, and label the knot "my ferocious editor." Recognize that it's the job of your ferocious editor to keep you from making bad mistakes. Sometimes your ferocious editor does a legitimate job, like when it keeps you from mouthing off to a cop or telling your loved one what you *really* think about that new haircut. But your ferocious editor has its own false assumptions. It assumes that it knows what a bad mistake is, and further believes that it's always acting in your best interest. Your ferocious editor simultaneously underestimates your chances for success and overestimates the penalty for failure. Tell your ferocious editor to go to hell.

Easier said than done, right? After all, your ferocious editor is a strong-willed sumbitch. Plus, I have presented this useful fiction that your ferocious editor is somehow a force of opposition, and not really part of you at all, but we know better, don't we? Your ferocious editor is *you*, and how do you fight you?

Later, when we're talking about making good jokes better, or rewriting to comic effect, or polishing your gems, we will bring the ferocious editor back to life. We'll welcome him in and say, "Now. Now is your chance to be demanding and unrelenting in pursuit of quality. Go for it, ferocious editor, for you are my best friend." But here, in this early stage, we really need to silence that voice, neutralize that cranial bully who wants its fears to be your fears. To kill your ferocious editor, you'll need weapons. The *rule of nine* is one of my favorites.

THE RULE OF NINE

For every ten jokes you tell, nine will be trash. For every ten ideas you have, nine won't work. For every ten times you risk, nine times you fail.

Depressing? Not really. In fact, the rule of nine turns out to be highly liberating because once you embrace it, you instantly and permanently lose the toxic expectation of succeeding every time. It's that expectation and the consequent fear of failure that give your ferocious editor such power over you. Remove the expectation and you remove the power. Simple, clean; a tool.

But wait, isn't there a contradiction here? Didn't I just say that you can't assume success *or* failure? Didn't I say you won't know until you try? Then how the heck can I assume a dreadful and paltry 10% success rate for our comic endeavors? I can't, really. Fact is, I don't have a logical leg to stand on. I invoke the rule of nine not as a truism but as another useful fiction to help me in my never-ending battle against fear.

Maybe you think I'm splitting hairs. What, after all, is the difference between *fearing* failure and *assuming* failure? The answer lies in expectation. When you expect success, you fear failure. You have something to lose. However, with the rule of nine, your expectations start so low that you have very nearly nothing to lose.

But wait, there's more.

If you only expect one joke in ten to work, then it stands to certain reason that you'll need hundreds and hundreds of failed jokes to build a decent body of work. You'll have to try and fail and try and fail and try and fail, and try again, in order to reach the point of trying and not failing. By simple mathematical logic, you end up persuading yourself that the process of failure is vital to the product of success. This co-opts your ferocious editor; it's not dead yet, but maybe a little less bossy than before.

The rule of nine, then, is a tool for lowering expectations. Let's try it out and see how it works. Generate a list of ten funny names for sports teams. Remember, it's quantity, not quality, we're after here. In fact, to lower your expectations even more, try to complete the exercise in five minutes or less. This further works to convince your ferocious editor that nothing's at risk, nothing's on the line.

Later, we'll be able to attack this comic problem with a whole slew of tools. For now, though, just ask and answer this question: What would a funny name for a sports team be?

> The Memphis Mudskippers
> The Slaves to Alliteration
> The Hair Triggers
> The London Fog
> The L.A. Riot
> The New York Happy Cabbies
> The Fighting Dustmites
> The Mgpxrhgmerersters
> The Team with the Incredibly Long, Virtually
>   Unpronounceable, and Almost Impossible to
>   Work Into a Cheer Name

Not a particularly funny list, is it? But with the rule of nine, it doesn't have to be. All we're trying to do here is get used to writing things down, without risk or burden, expectation or fear. Now you try. We'll assume that you have a blank piece of paper or the back of an old envelope to write on. I'll be suggesting quite a few exercises throughout this book, and, while no one's holding a gun to your head, remember that the first step to mastering tools is getting a feel for the darn things. Maybe you should stock up now on old envelopes. Or you could always use a notebook or scrawl in the margins. Sometimes I'll leave some blank spaces on the page. Like I said, the first rule is that there are no rules.

Want to make your ferocious editor retreat some more? Do this:

LOWER YOUR SIGHTS

This makes no sense, right? After all, people are always telling us to raise our sights. True, but then people are always telling us that the check is in the mail, and they'll still respect us in the morning, and a six-jillion-dollar deficit is nothing to worry about, so we can't necessarily believe everything they say anyhow.

Whether you're a stand-up comic or a screenwriter or a novelist or a humorous essayist or a cartoonist or an artist or a greeting card writer or a public speaker or whatever, you're possibly burdened by the strong desire to be *very successful right now.* No sooner do I start writing this book, for example, than I catch myself wondering whether it will sell a lot of copies, get me on the talk show circuit, make me famous, and lead to other books, movie deals, and invitations to all the best parties. Sheesh, it's not even *published* yet.

And yet, right down here on the level of this sentence, I'm hoping that this book will make me a made guy. I really want to be a made guy, but as long as I dwell on what it's like to be *a made guy,* a winner, I can't concentrate on writing this book—the very thing I'm hoping will make me a made guy in the end. To mix a metaphor most heinously, here at square one I'm looking for pie in the sky. What in heaven's name do I do now?

I lower my sights. I concentrate on this chapter, this paragraph, this sentence, this phrase, this word. Why? Because hope of success can kill comedy just as surely as fear of failure. With the rule of nine, we attack our fear of failure. By lowering our sights, we attack our need for success.

I can't stress this point enough. Right now the only thing that matters is the task at hand. Concentrate on the task at hand and everything else will take care of itself.

Yeah, right, Pollyanna. Just do your homework and the book will get published, and the talk shows will call, and the money, the fame, the glory, the party invitations will magically fly in the window. Okay, maybe not. But this much you know to be true: If you *don't* concentrate on the task at hand, then the book (or play, or joke, or cartoon, or essay, or speech, or greeting card, or stand-up act) will never get finished, and you'll have no chance at the glory you want.

The comic process takes place one step at a time. Unless you're Superman, you can't leap tall buildings at a single bound, so it's really kind of stupid to tell yourself you must. Be aware of this stupidity. Require of yourself only that you do what you can do now. Do this one thing and your ferocious editor will melt like Frosty the proverbial Snowman.

Okay, now we have two tools that attack and diminish our process-killing fears: the rule of nine and lowering our sights. What other weapons can we bring to bear? This question, you may be pleased to learn, is not rhetorical.

POSITIVE REINFORCEMENT AS SELF-FULFILLING PROPHECY

Applaud every small victory, because every time you do, you create an environment in which a larger victory can grow.

Man, I like that thought. I'm going to repeat it for those in the back of the class. *Applaud small victories. They make big victories grow.*

Let's try another exercise and see if we can augment our efforts with positive reinforcement. First, using the rule of nine, write a list of ten funny names in your notebook. Here, I'll start you off:

Julianne Potatoes
Spenley Cruntchwhistle
Dan Quayle

Okay, now you go. I'll wait . . .

Dum de dum dum dum . . .

Nice day, huh?

A little smoggy, yeah, but that's . . . Done already? Good work.

Now how do you feel? If all went according to plan, you used the tool of lowering your sights to keep false expectations to a minimum. You recognized this as a simple, trivial, and very possibly pointless exercise, designed to do nothing more than limber up your comic muscles. You didn't expect it to change your life, and, hey presto!, it didn't.

Now use the rule of nine to scan your list and discover that, yup, most of these joke names really aren't all that funny. And suddenly that's okay, because according to the rule of nine, they don't have to be.

But what you did do is this very important thing: *you finished the exercise.* You got from point A to point B without wandering off into the never-never land of procrastination. You *did the job.* You did it no better nor worse than you expected to, and, in fact, you didn't expect to do it particularly well or badly at all. Thus unburdened, you got it done, which may be more than what's happened in the past.

So pat yourself on the back. Take the win.

Now look what happens: You congratulate yourself for doing this little job. That gives you a stronger sense of yourself as someone who can do a job. Which makes you slightly better equipped to do the job next time. Which means better performance next time. Which means improved self-image. Which means enhanced performance. Which means—well, you get the gist.

What we're doing here is watching positive reinforcement turn into self-fulfilling prophecy. The better you imagine yourself to be, the better you become.

Whoa, hey, there's a powerful concept, huh? *The better you imagine yourself to be, the better you become.* And how did you get better? By abandoning all interest in getting better in the first place. It's almost Zen, isn't it? You get better by not trying to get better. How is this possible?

You've changed your focus. You're concentrating on the *process*, not the *product*. By attending to the ongoing performance instead of the applause at the curtain to come, you change the game from one you can never win to one you must always win. In so doing, you ditch your ferocious editor once and for all, for how can it manipulate your expectations when suddenly your only goal is to *experience the process?*

If this sounds a little too new-agey for you, then let it slide for now. But as the chapters roll by, and the exercises get tougher, please just concentrate on getting them done. Insofar as possible, let questions of quality fall from your mind. Your performance will improve, I promise.

Process, not product. Focus on this. In other words,

CONCENTRATE ON THE TASK AT HAND

Creativity and competition sometimes intersect. Much as we try to avoid it, we can't help comparing ourselves to others and measuring our progress against theirs. It's natural, inevitable. And it needs to be dealt with.

Suppose you got a call from a friend who'd just been offered a gig you really wanted and knew you could do quite well. Even as you congratulated him, you might find yourself wondering *why him, why not me?*

And if that call came in the middle of your working day, it could kill your creative process. Jealousy, envy, despair . . . all these weird, negative feelings swirl through the mind in a corrupting black cloud. How can you be funny with all that *noise* in your heads?

You go back to the one thing you can control: words on the page, cartoons in the sketch pad, whatever. By concentrating on the task at hand, you squeeze that inevitable competitive rage out of your mind. Then, having finished a small chunk of work by dint of sheer stubbornness, you use your positive-reinforcement tool and say to yourself, "Hey, this chunk of work is not half bad. Sure, someone out there has a job I want, but at least I have *this* to feel good about."

And having found some darn thing to feel good about, you improve your self-image, reduce your anxiety, focus your concentration, and raise the level of your confidence. This makes it possible to attend to the next task at hand, the next joke or paragraph or drawing or audition or whatever.

This war is won in small battles. And the task-at-hand tool relies heavily on the difficult delusion that the outside world somehow doesn't exist. Now, you know and I know that that's not true. At the end of the day, when the jokes are all written, the cartoons all drawn, what-have-you, there are still bills to pay, and transmissions to fix, and crying babies in the neighborhood, and vanishing rain forests, and that nagging unresolved question of whether Leno is better than Letterman or not.

But none of that matters when you're in the zone.

When you're concentrating on the task at hand, the outside world truly does not exist. You get in a lick of good work, pat yourself on the back for that lick of good work, then, taking that win, press on to the next piece of work, better equipped than ever to win. Thus do the tools complement one another. Thus does the snake swallow its own tail.

Soon we'll be moving on to the concrete tools of comedy, the nuts-'n'-bolts structural stuff you probably bought this book for in the first place. You may think that those tools are the only ones that matter. You may think that I've wasted a lot of time and a lot of words to create an emotional environment in which those tools can be used without unhelpful expectations, positive, negative, or otherwise. Would it make you feel better to know that I'm getting paid by the word? That's the joke answer. The real answer is this: *Without the proper emotional grounding, the tools themselves are useless.*

Unless you first make a commitment to fight the fears which inhibit creativity, you won't be funny at all. You will have wasted your money on this book, except for perhaps a buck you'll recoup at some yard sale some day.

In sum, then, pitching forward on your face is not a bad thing, but a good thing. At least in *falling* forward you're *moving* forward, and moving forward is all that really matters. Remember that stairs get climbed one step at a time.

Now that we're all so giddily un-results-oriented, let's look at how we can get some damn fine results out of our toolbox. In other words, enough yakking, here comes the hardware . . .

3
THE COMIC PREMISE

The comic premise is the gap between comic reality and real reality.

Any time you have a comic voice or character or world or attitude that looks at things from a skewed point of view, you have a gap between realities. Comedy lives in this gap.

The comic premise in, for example, *Back to the Future* is the gap between the comic reality of that movie's 1950s world and the "real" reality of Marty McFly. To him, Ronald Reagan is President of the United States; to people living in the 1950s, Reagan's just a hack actor. That joke is typical of the film and reflects its comic premise.

In *Catch-22*, you can see the comic premise in the gap between Yossarian's world view, "I'm sane, but I want to be crazy," and everyone else's world view, "We're crazy, but pretend to be sane."

In the comic strip *Peanuts*, to take a wildly different example, there's a gap between Snoopy's "real" reality—he's a dog—and his comic reality—he's a World War I flying ace. You don't have to look at movies or books or even comic strips to find the gap of the comic premise. It's right down there at the level of the joke, the gag, the funny line.

> *"I haven't had sex in a year."*
> *"Celibate?"*
> *"No, married."*

The gap here is the difference between a real-world reason—

celibacy—and a comic-world reason—marriage—for not having had sex.

The comic premise exists in all comic structures, no matter how large or small. Even the lowly pun is a function of the gap between the "real" reality of the way you expect a certain word to behave and the comic reality of the way it ends up behaving in the joke.

> *A man walked up to me and said, "I haven't had a bite in a week." So I bit him.*

We expect the word "bite" to refer to food. That's the real reality. But when it suddenly refers to aggressive behavior instead, it twists into comic reality. That's the gap. See the gap. Be the gap. Use the Force, Luke.

The television series *Mork and Mindy* established the gap between the "real" reality of Mindy's world and the comic reality of Mork's. In *The Wonder Years*, it's the presence of a narrator, an adult looking back at his childhood, that motors the humor of that show. The gap here is between what a child knows and what an adult has learned from experience.

Can you find the comic premise in greeting cards? You bet your dollar forty-nine you can. Consider the following:

> *"A birthday toast to your best year ever!"*
> *and then you open the card . . .*
> *"1976, wasn't it?"*

Here the gap opens between the recipient's real reality, expectation of good wishes, and the sender's comic reality, an irony instead.

James Thurber's writings, to take a more high-school literature tack, often describe the gap, literally, between reality and fantasy, particularly a given character's comic fantasy interpretation of the reality around him. What's "The Secret Life of Walter Mitty" if not a cruise along the gap between Mitty's inner world and the outer world he refuses to acknowledge?

Even titles can express a comic premise. Suppose you encountered a mystery novel entitled *Spenley Cruntchwhistle, Private Eye*. Would you not expect this book to be a comic mystery or perhaps a children's book? If yes, it's because of the gap between real reality (serious novels, serious titles) and comic reality (a detective with a joke name).

Now you may think that this is a little over-analytical, but bear with me. Once you recognize the gap of the comic premise, you'll start to see it in every funny situation that crosses your path. And once you start to see it in everyday situations, you'll begin to reverse the process, not just seeing it in experienced situations but *investing it* in comic situations of your own construction. That's when the comic premise stops being a self-indulgent mental exercise and starts behaving like a tool.

Okay, so let's do it. Let's use the comic premise as a tool to create comic situations. In fact, we'll do it twice: once right now and again later in the chapter after we've broken the comic premise into its component parts. Down the left side of the page, write ten real realities. Then, down the right side of the page, write ten comic realities that conflict with them. Before you begin, remember that it's the process not the product that matters. You won't be graded, it won't go on your permanent record, and neatness doesn't count. In fact, all that really counts is getting the dang thing done as quickly as possible so we can push on. I'll do a few to get you started.

going to the store	shopping for Uzis
a cop stops a pickup truck	it's full of space aliens
the Magna Carta	written by e.e. cummings

Right away, we start looking for something unexpected to create the comic reality. In fact, one way to solve this problem is just to think about what is expected and then insert the opposite.

going to church	in the nude
high-school shop class	taught by Albert Einstein
listening to a symphony	dancing to a symphony

If you found this exercise easy, it's probably because you just let yourself go and allowed your flights of fancy to carry you away. Surprisingly, if you found the exercise tough, it may be because you didn't have quite enough structure around which to organize your thoughts.

The unstructured mind asks, "What's funny?" and instantly gets lost in a mass of amorphous goo. The somewhat structured mind focuses on this thing called the comic premise and tries to get led by some magic hand to some creative end. Less amorphous, but still goo. The more we structure the task, the more we convert the act of creation to the act of asking and answering simple questions, the easier the whole thing gets.

Within the comic premise, there's not just one gap between real reality and comic reality, but all sorts of different gaps. They all turn on *conflict*, and the deeper the conflict gets, the more interesting the premise becomes.

THREE TYPES OF COMIC CONFLICT

In classic dramatic structure, there are three types of conflict: man against nature, man against man, and man against self. Since comic conflict is often just dramatic conflict with laughs attached, it will come as no huge surprise that these three levels of conflict exist in comic structure, too. You'll find your comic premise on one, two, or all three levels of conflict.

The first type of comic conflict, so-called *global conflict*, is the conflict between people and their world. The conflict can be that of a normal character in a comic world or of a comic character in a normal world. Simple? Pedantic? Just wait!

A normal character in a comic world stands in for the reader or viewer or listener and represents real reality. The situation he finds himself in represents the comic reality. In *Back to the Future*, Marty McFly is a normal character in a comic world. Same with *Connecticut Yankee in King Arthur's Court*. Same with the cartoon character Ziggy. Same with Bill Cosby when he introduces us to his quirky friends, Fat Albert, Old Weird Harold, etc.

A comic character in a normal world, on the other hand, carries the comic premise with him. In *Tootsie*, when Michael Dorsey becomes Dorothy Michaels, he turns into a comic character. His world hasn't changed; his own act of transformation has created the comic premise.

When Robin Williams does stand-up comedy, he creates his humor by looking at the straight world in a bent way. Contrast this with Cosby, who looks at a bent world in a straight way. This is the difference between a comic character in a normal world and a normal character in a comic world.

Global conflict is often social conflict; that is, it pits an individual against a whole social structure. In *Stripes*, it's Bill Murray against the US Army. In *The Phil Silvers Show*, it's Sergeant Bilko against the US Army. In *Private Benjamin*, it's Goldie Hawn against the US Army. Does one get the impression that the US Army gets picked on? Well, they've been picking on us for years. In *Beverly Hills Cop*, it's Eddie Murphy versus the social elite. In *Mr. Smith Goes to Washington*, it's Jimmy Stewart versus politics-as-usual. This is global conflict.

So looking back at our last exercise, we can now refine it as follows: Create a comic situation that finds its premise in global conflict. You create a normal character, a businessman, say, and then you create a social structure against which to pit him. *Et voilà*: the IRS audit from hell.

Or reverse it. Let the IRS audit office be the normal world now, and let the comic character be one insanely belligerent (or insanely naive, or insanely stupid, or insanely anything) auditee. Later, we'll discuss how to get more punch out of these situations; for now, it's enough to know that this sort of conflict exists.

Create a few new comic premises built entirely on global conflict and see if the task isn't easier now that you've narrowed the focus. My money is on yes.

A bumbling scientist is at odds with a chemical firm
A renegade rock star turns against the music establishment
An average joe fights city hall
A town tackles an alien invasion
A teacher takes on the school board
A school falls prey to a quirky new principal

Notice that these conflicts aren't necessarily comic. That's okay. In a few chapters we'll have all the tools we need to turn any conflict into a comic one. For now, let's move on to the second type of conflict, *interpersonal* or *local conflict*, battles between individuals.

There are two types of local conflicts. One pits a comic character against a normal character, and the other finds comic characters in opposition. In both cases, the conflict is between people who have an emotional bond. They care about each other. This doesn't mean that they love each other, or even like each other. They may hate each other, but they clearly care. That's what separates this sort of conflict from the conflict between, say, a cop and a con artist. Like the ads say, "This time it's personal."

Mork and Mindy are perfect examples of a comic character versus a normal character. Mork's is the comic reality while Mindy's is real. The gap between their personalities is the comic premise of the show.

Felix and Oscar in *The Odd Couple*, on the other hand, are comic characters in opposition. Each has a strong comic reality, and these comic realities clash hard. This will be made clearer in the next chapter when we talk about comic characters and their strong comic perspectives.

It's nice when things fit into categories, but what about when things don't fit into categories? What about *What About Bob?* In this film, Richard Dreyfuss is a world-class shrink, and Bill Murray is a world-class loon. Normal character versus comic character, or comic characters in opposition? Who knows? More to the point, who cares?

The tool we're using here is called *classification*. It's a useful but tricky tool. Putting things into categories often helps one see the things more clearly . . . but push everything into pigeonholes and in the end all you get are squished pigeons. If a story or a show or a situation defies easy classification, don't sweat it. As we'll discover soon, the best comedy crosses lines of definition.

Let's tackle our comic premise exercise again, only this time create comic premises built on a comic character versus a normal character, and on comic characters in opposition. Our IRS example won't work now because that's a character versus a world, and the emotional investment is nil. But make the IRS agent the ex-wife of the businessman and you've got juicy local conflict.

> A normal guy deals with a crazy neighbor
> A soldier and a pacifist go to war
> An astronomer marries an astrologer
> A conservative father battles a liberal son
> A wild genius poses problems for her tutor
> A prude and a pimp join forces

Notice once again how much easier it is to make choices when you have more precise questions to ask. Start with the question, "What's a comic premise?" and you founder. But start with, "What's a conflict between a normal character and a comic character?" and you're already into specifics. You're moving toward detail.

Throughout this book, we'll make every effort to move from the general to the specific. Life is better there.

Not just in comedy but in all storytelling, the richest conflict is the conflict within. Sure, we have a passing interest in how Herman Munster fares on jury duty, and yes, we're vaguely curious about Felix and Oscar and that scratch in the dining-room table, but for true dramatic drive, nothing beats seeing characters at war with themselves.

In one sort of *inner conflict*, a normal character becomes a comic character, and the comedy is rooted in the character's change of state. In *Tootsie*, Michael Dorsey starts out as a man and becomes a woman. He's a normal character as a man and a comic character as a woman. The movie turns on the conflict between his normal and his comic selves. Likewise, the Tom Hanks character in *Big*. He starts off normal—a kid—and becomes comic— a kid in an adult's body.

It's also possible to have a comic character at war with himself without his undergoing a change of state. Murphy Brown is a creature filled with doubt. Her doubt was with her long before we met her, and it will be with her long after we're gone. That's inner conflict.

So to couch the comic premise in terms of inner conflict, we might explore the story of a sighted man who goes blind, or that of a blind guy who won't admit that he can't see.

It's easiest to view inner conflict in terms of a normal character who undergoes a comic transformation. And you can make this happen by taking any character and turning him into his opposite. Man into woman, child into adult, idiot into genius, etc.

> A kid becomes a CEO
> A housewife becomes a NATO commander
> The President of Paraguay becomes a boxboy at the A&P
> A classical pianist becomes a rock goddess
> A prince turns into a frog
> A gnome becomes a fashion model
> A football player becomes a ballet star

The really interesting thing about these three types of conflict is how they connect and interleave. In the best comic storytelling, all three types are present in the same situation. When Walter Mitty disappears into fantasy, he is a comic character in a normal world, but he also has conflict with loved ones, and he has conflict within himself over the role he plays.

Or to take another example, in the movie *Trading Places*, Dan Aykroyd and Eddie Murphy do a prince-and-pauper number and become each other. They have global conflict—each struggles to survive in his new and challenging world. They also have local conflict with one another and with the people around them, people they love or hate or rage against or fear. Plus, they each have inner conflict, the struggle of a normal character who has, by transformation, become a comic character and struggles to come to terms with his new persona.

In your comic premises, you should strive for situations that exploit all three types of comic conflict. These situations will reliably be the most richly rewarding comic earth you till. If you aren't sold on my examples, simply take a moment to think of your favorite stand-up comics or movies or television shows or books or cartoons. Don't you enjoy the complex ones more than the simple ones?

In *Calvin and Hobbes*, Calvin has global conflict (teachers, parents, space aliens, and other authority figures), and local conflict (Hobbes), and inner conflict (uncontrollable flights of fancy). Nancy and Sluggo, on the other hand, battle the world and each other, but they never battle themselves. Which is the more interesting strip?

A stand-up comic might do a routine about bad airplane food, and it might be very funny. But if she makes it so that the flight attendant is an old enemy who's trying to poison her, and paints herself as a horrible acrophobe who never should have flown in the first place, then the material, so to speak, can really take off.

Try this exercise: Imagine that you've been given the chance to draw a comic strip for a national syndicate. (Can't draw? Never mind; neither can I, but let's pretend, shall we?) Attack this problem in terms of the comic premise: What sorts of comic conflict would make for fun comic strips?

A long-suffering schoolteacher copes with her holy terrors
Newlyweds struggle with in-laws, each other, and
    themselves
A boy has a pot-bellied pig for a pet
A quick-witted sheriff runs a county jail
A single mother and her teenage daughters can't get along
A typical suburban family moves to a space station
A cartoonist can't keep his characters from coming to life

You may have noticed that I try to keep my comic premises short, the length of a sentence or less. Like they say, brevity is the soul of wit; more to the point, it's the soul of understanding. If you can't boil your comic premise down to a single line, the chances are that you don't quite have a handle on it yet. Move toward simplicity; if nothing else, it means less work for you when you're using the rule of nine to separate the wheat from the voluminous chaff.

One final thought before we continue: The comic premise not only creates comedy, it also casts the light of truth on a given situation. Specifically, the comic reality reveals the truth in the "real" reality. When Snoopy pretends he's a World War I flying ace, he's revealing an essential truth: *people pretend.* Going back to our notion of truth and pain, look to your normal characters to reveal the meaning of your comic premise, and look to your comic characters to reveal its humor. When Dustin Hoffman rips off his wig at the end of *Tootsie*, the comic character (Dorothy) gets the laughs, but the normal character (Michael) demonstrates the truth and pain: Men and women behave badly toward one another— unless they learn.

To recap: The comic premise is the gap between real reality and comic reality. Every form of humor, from the smallest joke to the largest comic tale, has some sort of defining gap or comic conflict. There are three types of comic conflict: Global conflict takes place between an individual and his world. Local conflict is about people fighting people; you always hurt the one you love. Inner conflict features a character at war with himself. Inner conflict is always the richest and most rewarding. Just ask Hamlet, or any other comic character.

Oh, you don't buy Hamlet as a comic character? Well, maybe I can change your mind . . .

4
COMIC CHARACTERS

You know what a comic character is, right? That guy sitting behind you at the baseball game who, after six or seven beers, feels he has a personal, adversarial relationship with the umpire or the manager or the visiting pitcher, and a divinely ordained right to share the intimacies of these relationships at the top of his lungs with everyone around him. This person is a comic character right up until the moment he spills a cold beer down your back. Then he's just a jerk.

Okay, seriously, when I say "comic character," who springs to your mind? Lucille Ball, Groucho Marx, Charlie Chaplin, Charlie Brown, Lily Tomlin, Johnny Carson, Ziggy, Bart Simpson, Joel Fleischman, Bertie Wooster, Jonathan Winters, Robin Williams, Sissy Hankshaw, Dave Barry, etc., etc. In truth, you can't swing a dead cat in popular culture without hitting an authentic comic character. Which does you not much good in creating your own comic characters, does it?

Fear not. As your faithful comic alchemist, I have found a formula for creating comic characters. It's not quite as elegant as spinning gold from dross, but a darn sight more reliable. By the end of this chapter, you'll be able to build comic characters of your own, from scratch, in about two minutes flat. In Frankensteinian fashion, you'll have created a monster.

Not all of your comic characters will be "keepers," solid, memorable creations that can stand the weight of major development. But you know me, ol' Johnny Rule-of-Nine. In my universe, it's necessary to create lots and lots and lots of comic characters before I can be confident of having a chosen few who show real quality and promise. So what I'm after for my own creative purposes—and what I'd like to share with you now—is a comic assembly line, if you will, that can churn out bunches of comic characters. Then we'll set 'em loose and see which ones perform.

Four elements go into the construction of a comic character. The first and most important is the comic perspective.

THE COMIC PERSPECTIVE

Show me a comic character without a comic perspective and I'll show you a straight man.

The heart and soul of any comic character is his STRONG COMIC PERSPECTIVE. I repeat these words—STRONG COMIC PERSPECTIVE—and capitalize them because they may be the three most important words in this book. Every comic character begins and ends with his strong comic perspective. Know this one thing about your characters and you'll know what makes them consistently and reliably funny forever.

The comic perspective is a character's unique way of looking at his world, which differs in a clear and substantial way from the "normal" world view. In the last chapter, I talked about the comic premise as the gap between real reality and comic reality. In a sense, the comic perspective is a character's own individual comic premise. The comic perspective functions in a character exactly as the comic premise functions in a story: It defines the gap that the laughs will spark across.

Gracie Allen's comic perspective was innocence. It was the filter through which she looked at the world, and through which her humor flowed. Harpo Marx's comic perspective was playfulness. Groucho's, on the other hand, was, shall we say, leering cynicism. In *Northern Exposure*, Joel Fleischman's comic perspective is, basically, "New York rules, Alaska bites." Can you see that every funny thing that happens to him on that show is a function of his comic perspective?

Jerry Lewis, in his movie heyday, had a bumbler's perspective. He acted clumsy but, more importantly, *thought* clumsy. Jack Benny's comic perspective was *tightwad*. (Tightwaddishness?

Tightwadditry? The noun escapes me.) The classic Jack Benny bit has a robber telling Jack, "Your money or your life." When Jack answers, "I'm thinking . . ." he's filtering the robber's threat through his strong comic perspective. The possibility that Jack might value his life less than his money is what creates the laugh. And it's his comic perspective that brings that possibility to life.

A character's strong comic perspective is the motor that drives his comic engine. Comedy flows from character, which really means that comedy flows from a character's unique, quirky, off-beat way of looking at the world. When I see a great stand-up comic, what I admire most is his or her ability to take the ordinary details of everyone's life and see them in a new and different light. Jerry Seinfeld has a knack for magnifying the minutiae of modern life; Jimmy Durante looked at the world through nose-colored glasses.

Notice that I speak of a *strong* comic perspective. You will find in creating your own comic perspectives (which you'll be doing in about thirty seconds from now) that the stronger they are, the funnier they are. It's a direct mathematical function. You could graph it.

Okay, so now we have a new tool called *comic perspective*. Let's put it to work by generating ten strong ones. I'll go first.

> virginal schoolboy
> newborn baby
> curmudgeonly oldster
> hard-luck loser
> space alien
> cockeyed optimist
> testosterone poisoning
> canny politician
> perfectly paranoid
> know-it-some

Each of these is a single, clearly defined way of looking at the world. A virginal schoolboy, for example, would see a woman's naked breast as the bridge to manhood, while a newborn baby would see the same breast as . . . lunch! The know-it-some will tell you that the submarine sandwich was invented by the Earl of Submarine; the perfectly paranoid person will wonder if it's poisoned. Virtually anything can be filtered through a comic perspective, and virtually any point of view can be a comic perspective. Give it a go.

It's likely that you don't love all your perspectives. Some of them may seem flat, dull, unpromising. Why is this? If you examine your list, I think you'll find that the boring comic perspectives are the ones that travel the least distance from commonly held perspectives. A priest's perspective, for example, is not inherently funny. Something must be done to that perspective, something that pushes it toward some edge and wedges open the gap between what's real and what's funny. That something is *exaggeration*, the tool we'll check out next.

Before we go, though, I'd like you to look briefly at your own creative process. By this point in the voyage, if you're starting to get the hang of using tools, then your ideas should be flowing a little more freely, both as a function of changed expectation, and as a function of finer focus. Notice how the problems we're solving continue to get increasingly smaller. (Bonus points to you who said, "Whoa, check that oxymoron.")

We started out asking, "What's funny?" Then we asked, "What's a funny story?" Then we asked, "What's a comic character in a funny story?" Now we're asking, "What's a comic character's strong comic perspective?" Next we'll ask, "How can we make that strong comic perspective even stronger still?"

EXAGGERATION

If you can't be right, be loud.

The thing about Gracie Allen is not just that she was innocent but that she was the ultimate innocent. No one could possibly be more naive than Gracie. Likewise, no one could possibly be a bigger bumbler than Jerry Lewis (with the possible exception of Peter Sellers' Inspector Clouseau.) There's no confusing Mork's or ALF's alien perspective with anything from around here. They came—literally—from millions of miles away.

The tool of exaggeration, then, simply takes a comic perspective and pushes and stretches and accelerates it until it's sufficiently far from our perspective that it starts to be funny. A priest's perspective isn't necessarily funny, but if you turn him into a perpetual sot, or into the ultimate twinkly-eyed rascal, you start to move him where you want him to go.

This tool, exaggeration, above all else, requires that you *be bold*. We writers tend to think in terms of what's logical, but comedy defies logic. What's dynamic? What's strange? WHAT IS WRIT LARGE? That's what we're going for here. Joel Fleischman is compelling because he's so strongly drawn. It's not that he kinda likes New York and sorta doesn't like Alaska. It's rather that he unreservedly *loves* New York and utterly *loathes* Alaska. Nothing less would do.

The rule, then, is this: Take your comic character's comic perspective *to the end of the line*. When Dudley Moore played a drunk in *Arthur*, he was the drunkest drunk the world had seen (since Falstaff). Woody Allen isn't just neurotic; as a comic character, he's a Freudian field day. I'm beating a dead horse about this, I know, but it's key, so bear with me. Most failed comic characters fail as a function of their limited exaggeration. Would Robin Williams be less interesting and less fun if he were less totally manic? You bet your two-drink minimum he would.

More examples: remember Goldie Hawn in *Laugh-In?* She wasn't just a ditzy airhead, she was the ultimate ditzy airhead. That's what made her funny. Walter Mitty doesn't fantasize about catching a bus on time, he fantasizes saving the world. Thurber took Mitty's comic perspective to the limit. That's what you must do.

You know, I've talked a lot about not being afraid to fail, and I'm going to say it again here: When you attempt to exaggerate a comic character, don't be afraid to fail. Because here's the good news: In this case, you *can't* fail. There's no such thing as exaggerating too much. Isn't that a blessing?

Exaggerating.

Exagggerating.

Exagggerating. Too much!

All right, let's try another exercise. This time we want to take a comic perspective and push it to its limit. If your character's comic perspective, for example is, *she likes cats*, then an exaggeration of that would be *feline-obsessed; has twelve dozen of them*. If the comic perspective is *parental disapproval*, the exaggeration is *hates everything kids do, from their music to their food to the little lights they have in their shoes these days*. Let's look at a list.

Comic Perspective	Exaggeration
fearful	jumps at shadows
joyful	all manic all the time
drunk	stewed to the gills
thrill seeker	adrenaline junkie
eccentric collector	accumulation of nose hairs
tone deaf	Roseanne Barr

Tackle this one like those old SAT questions: A is to B as C is to ___.

Comic Perspective	Exaggeration

Exaggeration, by the way, is a tool that pays dividends all over the comic world, and we'll come back to it again and again. For now, though, let's look at the third facet of a comic character's construction, something without which no comic character would be complete . . . flaws.

FLAWS

What's wrong with this picture?

A comic character is funny as a function of his flaws. Flaws are failings or negative qualities within a person's attributes or aspects. In *Cheers*, Sam Malone's egomania is a flaw and Diane Chambers' snobbishness is a flaw. In P.G. Wodehouse's works, Bertie Wooster's fecklessness is a flaw, and his butler Jeeves's fastidious-ness is likewise a flaw. Hamlet's indecision is a flaw. My lack of speling skils is a fla.

Flaws in a comic character work to open emotional distance between a comic character and viewers or readers so that those viewers or readers can comfortably laugh at, say, someone slip-ping on a banana peel. Without this emotional distance, the truth and the pain of a situation hit too close to home for an audience to find funny. A thing is only funny if it happens to the other guy, and flaws in a character work to make him "the other guy" in a reader's or viewer's mind. When I freaked out over Leslie Parker in seventh grade, my flaw of indiscretion (and massive stupidity) separated me from my audience (the sadistic weasels) and allowed them to laugh at my discomfort in comfort. Oh joy.

Sometimes flaws are subjective; one man's flaw is another man's social outrage. In the film *A Fish Called Wanda*, the Michael Palin character was a stutterer. To some people that was a comic flaw. To others it was abusive. And unfunny. Remember that a joke always takes place in the context of an audience's expectations. When assigning flaws to your comic characters, you must always keep in mind what your audience will accept, tolerate, or just plain get. Also remember that a physical attribute can be a flaw with-out being a bad thing. Baldness, shortness, tallness, fatness, skinniness, excessive nose hair . . . these all work to distance the comic character from the audience: Whoever that guy is, he's nothing like me.

The more flaws you can find for your comic characters, the more interesting and complex and funny those characters will become. Al Bundy on *Married . . . with Children* is sloppy, sexist and selfish. He also has smelly feet and excessive nose hair. Louie DePalma on *Taxi* is venal, corrupt, lecherous, mean-spirited, etc. A comic character, in at least one sense, is the sum of his flaws.

A flaw can also be a positive aspect that's taken too far. Kindness, love, a giving or a trusting nature all turn into flaws when exaggeration makes them abnormal simply by writing them large. Charlie Brown's trusting nature is a flaw because he trusts too much. This lets us laugh when Lucy pulls that football away for the umpteen zillionth time.

Just as you can build a comic character from his comic perspective outward, so can you with his flaws. Find a flaw and you've found a comic character.

Hey, there's a mind-boggler, huh? *Find a flaw and you've found a comic character.* If this is true, then you could go to a simple list of nouns, pick ones that appeal to you, and use them as little comic launching pads. How hard can it be to find a noun?

Comedy is tools. If you have the right tools, you never have to stumble through the mirror-house of unfocused writing. It's a powerful thought. Perhaps we should all meditate on it for a moment, hmm?

Hmmmmmmmm-mmmmmmmmm-mmmmmmmmm-mmmmmmmmm.

Okay, back to work.

Greed is a flaw; Scrooge is a character. Wild abandon is a flaw; John Belushi is a character. Drunkenness is a flaw; Dean Martin is a character. Laziness is a flaw; Andy Capp is a character. Stubbornness is a flaw; Murphy Brown is a character.

To see this relationship more clearly, take a moment to generate a list of flaws and then extrapolate an appropriate comic character for each one. It should all look something like this:

Flaw	Comic Character
fearfulness	multiphobic weenie
insecurity	nervous nelly
dementia	psycho killer
envy	covetous co-worker
drug abuse	total stoner
artificial leg	world's worst hurdler
fecklessness	silly uncle
baldness	wannabe sex symbol

It's not quite as easy as one-two-three. To generate this list, you have to go "shopping" in your head for appropriate nouns to put in column one and then find characters to link them to in column two. But isn't it a darn sight easier to think of mere words than to think of whole comic notions? You could even flip through a dictionary. None dare call it cheating.

Also notice that it's not necessary to link flaws to an "appropriate" character. It's logical, for example, to assign prudishness to a schoolmarm, but what if you assign that flaw to a stripper instead? An air-traffic controller? President of the United States? The possibilities are endless.

Sometimes flaws and comic perspective complement one another. Diane Chambers has the strong comic perspective of a drawing-room intellectual and the complementing flaw of snobbishness. Gracie Allen's comic perspective is innocence, which is a flaw as well. But what you really want is a kind of synergy between flaws and perspective so that some flaws conflict with the perspective while others reinforce it. Lucille Ball's comic perspective, "There's nothing I can't do," is aided by her flaw of impulsiveness, and thwarted by her flaw of incompetence. In the best comic characters, flaws and perspective go to war.

Think about this in terms of inner conflict. When a character is at war with himself, there's a sort of psychic no-man's land between where he is and where he wants to be. Flaws reflect his true nature; comic perspective is his fantasy self-image. Here, then, is another comic premise you can exploit, the *inner comic premise*, the gap between how a character sees himself and who he really is. This doesn't hold true for all comic characters. Think of it as an angle you can sometimes play.

Fantasy	Reality
war hero	4-F weakling
beauty queen	plain jane
genius	stupid
loved by all	loner

Flaws, then, serve two purposes: They create conflict within characters, and they create emotional distance between character and audience. Having created this distance, oddly, it's now necessary to remove it. That's where humanity comes in, the fourth and final facet of a comic character.

HUMANITY

I like him; he's like me.

We used flaws to drive a wedge between the character and the audience so that the audience could laugh. Now we use humanity to build a bridge between the character and the audience so that the audience can care.

Story-structure gurus will tell you that it's vital for an audience to care. The central character or hero of any successful story, they'll tell you, must arouse in the reader's or the viewer's mind both sympathy and empathy. That is, you're supposed to like the hero, and he's supposed to be like you. If that happens, you engage emotionally with the hero and gladly undertake his quest with him; you care.

The same is true with comic characters, and logically so. After all, if you want to find someone consistently funny for the life of a story, you'd better feel a part of his experience somehow. So what it comes down to is this: In some way, all comic characters have *humanity*. If they don't, we don't care. It's as simple as that.

Simple, yes, but why? Remember that comedy is truth and pain so that without some means of connecting a comic character's truth to our own experience, we have no way of knowing what we're supposed to find funny. A character's humanity is the bridge we need. Recall the difference between a class clown and a class nerd. The class clown was funny because his experience was your experience. The class nerd was an object of scorn and derision because he stood apart; you couldn't relate. In the cruel Darwinian quicksand of junior-high school, the nerd had no humanity.

So what is humanity, anyhow? Can we look at a creep like Dan Fielding on *Night Court* and find his humanity? You bet your inflatable rubber love-doll we can. Sure, he's a slime bucket, venal, sexist, corrupt, all of that. But when push comes to shove, he'll do the right thing, even if it means giving up his smarmy goals. That's a classic definition of humanity: He'll do the right thing in a pinch. Louie DePalma has the same humanity. But of course that's not the only kind of humanity.

Look at Otto in *A Fish Called Wanda*. What is his humanity? He's a romantic. He has a romantic soul. We forgive him his flaws, and root for his cause, because secretly he's a romantic, and secretly so are we all.

Here are some comic good guys and their humanity: Charlie Brown is vulnerable. Robin Williams is energetic. Jonathan Winters is a teddy bear. Goldie Hawn is bubbly. Lily Tomlin is insightful. Arnold Schwarzenegger is strong. Hannibal Lecter is charming . . .

Hey, hold on, hang on, Hannibal Lecter is a comic good guy? Hannibal the Cannibal from *Silence of the Lambs?* How could he be a good guy? For that matter, how could he be a comic character at all? Well, let's take a closer look.

Hannibal Lecter's strong comic perspective is "People are food." His flaws include arrogance, malevolence, psychotic behavior, no self-awareness, immorality, amorality, overwhelming evil, and really bad eating habits. He probably does not floss.

To be a comic character, he'll need a mountain of humanity to counterbalance his flaws. His positive qualities include intelligence, urbanity, poise, wit, good manners, loyalty to his friends, a sense of fair play, self-confidence, and an incredibly strong will to win: He'll stop at nothing to eat your face. Even as we abhor his flaws, his humanity makes us like him and want him to win.

To make Hannibal Lecter work on a comic level, it was necessary first to make him disgusting, make us revile him, and then pile on the humanity to counteract our revulsion. It's almost physics: For every flaw, there is an equal and opposite humanity. The worse you make some aspects of a comic character, the better you must make others.

One of the surest ways to create humanity is to give your comic character an indomitable will. No character is more compelling, more engaging, than the one who will stop at nothing to achieve his goal.

Be careful in assigning humanity. It's not enough to say of a character, "Sure, he's a hit man, but he loves his mother so he's okay." A character's humanity must be a real part of his character. If it's pasted on, you get a cartoon and not a character.

Also be aware that a character's flaw can also be part of his humanity. Lucy's impulsiveness, which always gets her into trouble, also makes us love her more. Mork's innocence creates distance and closeness at the same time.

Humanity, then, is the sum of a character's positive human qualities that inspire either sympathy or empathy or both. A list of such qualities might include:

    loyalty
    honesty
    generosity
    humility
    sense of humor
    curiosity
    vulnerability
    strength of will
    innocence

patience
physical strength
physical beauty

Or, a list of such qualities might include . . .

Now our picture of the comic character is complete: strong comic perspective, flaws, humanity, and exaggeration.

Comic Perspective is the unique world-view, at variance with normal reality, that motors the character's comic engine.

Flaws are the elements of a comic character that separate him from "real" people. If he has no flaws, he's generic. If he's generic, he's not funny.

Humanity is the quality of a comic character that unites him with the audience. Building sympathy and empathy, humanity lets us care.

Exaggeration is the force that works on all three—comic perspective, flaws, and humanity—to move a normal character further and further into the comic world. Exaggeration widens the gap upon which the comic premise of the character is built.

Let's look at some famous comic characters now and track their comic perspective, flaws, humanity, and exaggeration.

> Groucho Marx is a leering cynic, whose massive misanthropy is counteracted by his unbridled wry wit.
> Sam Malone, that wild egomaniac, is supremely sexist, but when he reveals his insecurity, we all fall in love.
> Diane Chambers is a hyperintellectual whose snobbishness is not attractive, but whose generosity of spirit is.
> Charlie Brown is a perennial loser. His self-pity would alienate us were it not for his long-suffering patience.

> Bertie Wooster views the world through the prism of privilege. His flaw is his classist attitude, but at least he knows how to accept help when he needs it.
>
> Jerry Lewis is bumbling and incompetent, yet sincere.
>
> Hamlet, that wacky Dane, is vengeful and indecisive, yet noble, strong-willed, and loyal to his dad.

It might be useful for you to do a few more on your own. Jack Benny? Charlie Chaplin? Lenny Bruce? The Tin Man? Mike Doonesbury?

You'll notice that it's possible for a comic character to have many comic perspectives, flaws, and human qualities. You want this. You want your comic characters to be interesting, complex, dynamic people full of rich potential for inner conflict, and this only happens when you build their personalities in layers. But for the purposes of simple comic construction, you don't have to go any further than hitting the marks: comic perspective, flaws, humanity, exaggeration.

I promised at the top of the chapter that by the end of it you'd be able to build comic characters with assembly-line speed, if not precision. Try it now. Create some comic characters. Give them names, comic perspectives, flaws, humanity, exaggeration.

As you do this exercise, look for lines of conflict between and among your categories. If you create a character whose comic perspective is fearlessness, for instance, go out of your way to assign phobias as a flaw and a superhero's desire to serve others as a humanity. This dynamic inner conflict will mean that some part of your character must naturally be wrong when everything else is right. Like Hamlet, he'll never be at peace.

To take another example, if your character's comic perspective is "love conquers all," give him selfishness as a flaw and guilelessness as humanity. This synergy will put such a character in a painful box, and a painful box is exactly where you want your comic characters to be.

CHARACTER: Spenley Cruntchwhistle
COMIC PERSPECTIVE: expert on everything
FLAWS: know-it-all attitude, massive holes in his
      knowledge
HUMANITY: well-meaning, sincere, helpful
EXAGGERATION: knows the seven chief exports
      of Bulgaria

CHARACTER: Ophelia Barnette
COMIC PERSPECTIVE: body is a temple of the holy spirit
FLAWS: shyness, smoldering libido
HUMANITY: loyal to her friends, desperately wants love
EXAGGERATION: undresses in the dark, even when alone

CHARACTER: Peter the Puppy
COMIC PERSPECTIVE: born to chew shoes
FLAWS: curiosity, no bladder control, sharp teeth
HUMANITY: playful, affectionate, soft and cuddly
EXAGGERATION: pees every five minutes

CHARACTER:
COMIC PERSPECTIVE:
FLAWS:
HUMANITY:
EXAGGERATION:

CHARACTER:
COMIC PERSPECTIVE:
FLAWS:
HUMANITY:
EXAGGERATION:

CHARACTER:
COMIC PERSPECTIVE:
FLAWS:
HUMANITY:
EXAGGERATION:

CHARACTER:
COMIC PERSPECTIVE:
FLAWS:
HUMANITY:
EXAGGERATION:

People are always asking me how to make a script funny, or a scene, or a story, or even a single line. People stop me in the supermarket. They say, "Hey mister, I can tell just by looking at you what a funny guy you are. How can I be funny, too?" The answer, I tell them as I tell you, is to invent characters, invest them with strong comic perspectives and flaws and humanity, exaggerate those attributes, then turn these creatures loose upon the world. Then I ask them if they know what aisle the peas are on.

If you want to be more consistently funny, start building a library of comic perspectives and start noticing how almost every joke or funny situation you encounter is a function of someone's comic perspective.

> As the husband said to his wife, "I can think for
> myself—can't I, dear?"

The husband's strong comic perspective is clear: The decision of the wife is final. His flaws and humanity are implied: He's meek, yet loyal to the woman he loves.

Which raises an interesting question: What is your strong comic perspective? How do you look at the world in a way that is unique, exaggerated, and at far variance from normal reality?

The first time I asked myself this question, I was wandering around a casino in Las Vegas, taking endless delight in the pit bosses and the poker players and the blue-haired slot-machine queens and the change girls and the gakky carpet and the noise and the lights and everything. I almost imagined that they'd built the whole darn casino just for me. With a flash of revelation, it hit me that this was my strong comic perspective: The world is my circus. Everything I see or hear or experience, everything that happens anywhere on earth, is just for my amusement. There's a guy in Colombia who considers it his mission in life to grow great beans for my coffee. DJs play my favorite songs without my having to ask. The IRS would never audit *my* taxes, unless they thought I'd get a kick out of the experience.

Of course this is an exaggeration, and of course I don't carry this attitude with me everywhere I go. But when I need a comic perspective, it's useful to have "the world is my circus" handy. At least I know where my next joke is coming from. Take a moment to ponder your own strong comic perspective. You don't have to settle on one, and you can always change your answer later, but if you're trying to be funny, it's useful to know what part of your personality already is funny.

Find your comic perspective and you have found your comic voice, the platform on which your humor can reliably and consistently stand from now until the day you die. Maybe even beyond.

Beyond? Oh, yes. Consider W.C. Fields. His strong comic perspective was that of a gruff curmudgeon. With the words on his tombstone, "On the whole, I'd rather be in Philadelphia," his comic perspective transcended his own death. That, folks, is a *strong* comic perspective.

5
SOME TOOLS FROM THE TOOLBOX

There's such a thing as delivering on the promise of a title. If I go see a movie called, for example, *Bill and Ted's Excellent Adventure*, I expect, if nothing else, an excellent adventure, and I'll be disappointed if the movie doesn't deliver the goods. Likewise, a TV show called *Family Ties* figures to deal in some way with family life. Either that or some odd bondage thing. James Thurber's story *The Defenestration of Erminitrude Inch* promises that someone will get thrown out of a window.

Every title makes a promise, and the film or show or book or cartoon strip or one-man mime troupe that fails to deliver on that promise risks losing its audience altogether.

As an exercise, spend a few minutes brainstorming titles for situation comedies and ask yourself what sort of promise your title implies.

Out of Her League, for instance, might suggest a long-suffering, sympathetic female lead who has trouble coping with the challenges of work and family and a 1975 Dodge Dart that stubbornly refuses to start.

Our Hundred Years' War promises some sort of domestic struggle, probably between an old married couple who have been loving and hating each other since roughly the dawn of time.

New Glorx in Town pledges a story about something called a Glorx and his or her or its efforts to adapt to a new and challenging environment.

What we have here is another back-door route to comic brainstorming. Instead of thrashing randomly for inspiration, we can simply generate a list of titles, ask what promise each title makes, and then develop the most promising premises among them.

Okay, so now here comes a book called *The Comic Toolbox: How to be Funny Even if You're Not.* What promises does that title make? That you'll be funnier going out than you were coming in. That you'll get a laugh or two along the way. And that you'll get some tools. If you don't, sooner or later you'll break faith with me and go back to watching *New Glorx in Town* or whatever the heck you were doing before. Well, the fact is we've used some of these tools already, but the time has come to start naming names.

CLASH OF CONTEXT

Clash of context is the forced union of incompatibles. Clash of context takes something from its usual place and sticks it where it doesn't fit in. A hooker in a convent is clash of context. So is an elephant in a bathtub. So is a new Glorx in town.

Northern Exposure takes Joel Fleischman out of his normal context, New York, and places him in the new and challenging world of Cecily, Alaska. *Crocodile Dundee* takes its title character out of his normal outback context and dumps him in New York.

There's a newspaper ad for hair transplants with the headline, "Flirt With Confidence." If you cut the headline from the hair transplant ad and paste it on the impotence ad on the next page, that's clash of context.

Consider song lyrics. They make sense within their context, but take them out of context—speak them or write them down—they can look fairly strange and comical indeed:

> *My name is Lenny Lunghead, I'm a fan of nicotine.*
> *I been smoking cigarettes since I was seventeen.*
> *You ask my why I do it,*
> *There's really nothing to it.*
> *I smoke 'cause I like to cough.*

Clash of context works at all levels of comedy, from broad

storytelling to simple verbal wordplay. It can be the premise of a comic novel, like *Gulliver's Travels*, or of a comic film, such as *Big*, in which Tom Hanks is taken out of his normal childhood context and placed into the foreign context of adulthood. Clash of context drives such TV shows as *The Beverly Hillbillies* (country folks in the city) and *Green Acres* (city folks in the country). You can build a sight gag on clash of context, like the final moment in *City Slickers*, when Billy Crystal shows up back in New York with a calf in his car. Clash of context tells jokes: *Marry in haste, repent in Reno.* Oxymorons are little clashes (clashlets? clashettes?) of context: honest larceny; drowning in the fountain of youth; television reality.

Clash of context, then, works by moving a thing from where it belongs to where it doesn't. And there are so many more places where a thing doesn't belong than where it does. For instance, a wedding is typically held in a church or a park or a private home. Where would a wedding typically *not* be held? How about a car wash or a pawn shop? In freeway traffic? Via computer? At a ball game? In a shopping mall? Clash of context turns out to be a surprisingly easy tool to use.

> kid president
> Albert Einstein in drag
> lunar golf course
> beauty pageant in prison
> Donald Trump on skid row
> Picasso painting velvet Elvises
> Madonna sings opera
> Michael Jackson versus Michael Tyson

Clash of context isn't always a physical juxtaposition; it can also be emotional or attitudinal juxtaposition, also known as . . .

THE WILDLY INAPPROPRIATE RESPONSE

In *Monty Python's Life of Brian*, there's a scene in which Brian is running for his life from Roman guards. He hides in a gourd shop where the shopkeeper browbeats him into haggling over the price of a cheap gourd. Here we have the shopkeeper's petty attitude played off against Brian's dire circumstance. This is clash of context expressed as a wildly inappropriate response.

Notice that you could turn the clash around and play off a dire attitude against a petty circumstance, like investing someone with a fear of heights so strong that she can't step off a curb without fainting. In fact, you can play off any attitude against any circumstance, so long as the attitude and the circumstance aren't naturally compatible. And the more incompatible they are, the funnier the scene or the joke or the notion will be.

If you see the tool of exaggeration at play here, slap a gold star on your forehead and go to the head of the class. We want a *wildly*, not a *mildly*, inappropriate response. You may also notice that a wildly inappropriate response is a function of a character's strong comic perspective. The gourd seller wants to haggle because his strong comic perspective tells him that haggling is God. It's okay that these tools overlap; an ocean is blue, but it's also wet.

The wildly inappropriate response is really pretty simple to use. Just pick a situation and ask yourself what the logical response to that situation would be. Then find the opposite of that response, or any of a host of other equally wrong answers, and you're in business.

Silent respect, for example, is appropriate to a funeral, so we go looking for noisy disrespect. Give all the mourners kazoos. Or tubas. Or automatic weapons.

Suppose you wrote a love scene in which the man asked the woman if it was good for her, too. If you wanted the woman to say yes in a comic way, you could have her hold up a card with the number 10 on it, like an Olympic judge. She would be using both an inappropriate response and a physical clash of context. Applying exaggeration to the scene, you'd end up with not just Olympic-style cards but actual physical Olympic judges (and the more the merrier!) in bed with the happy, loving couple.

Suppose you were an actor asked to improvise the following

set of scenes. How could you use the wildly inappropriate response to create a comic attitude to play within each scene?

Scene	Inappropriate Response
backyard barbecue	militant vegetarianism
at a baseball game	cheering for the vendors
death row	a giggle fit
firing an employee	sadistic delight
wedding night	vow of celibacy
at the beach	
church service	
scientific convention	
aerial combat	
in a nightclub	
asking for a date	
a television newscast	
fixing a car	
accepting an Oscar	
buying a computer	

When movie people talk about *high concept* ideas, they mean ideas that can be pitched and understood in a sentence or less. Often they end up talking clash of context: a boy in a man's body (*Big*); a man in women's clothing (*Tootsie*); a mermaid in Manhattan (*Splash*). Clash of context is a high-conceptician's best friend.

But it's cool to have more than one best friend, so let's check out another tool.

THE LAW OF COMIC OPPOSITES

To use this tool, first create a comic character and identify her or his strong comic perspective. Then seek the diametric opposite of that perspective and assign that opposite to a second character. Now lock them in a room together. Now sit back and watch the fun.

In *The Odd Couple*, Felix Unger is all anal all the time, and Oscar Madison is the crème de la slob. These are comic opposites, comic characters in opposition. In *Midnight Run*, Robert de Niro plays a super-rational bounty hunter and Charles Grodin is a world-class neurotic. For much of the movie, the two are literally handcuffed together. That's a forced union.

Humphrey Bogart and Katherine Hepburn are comic opposites in *The African Queen*, likewise trapped together by circumstance. If Gracie Allen is the ultimate naif, it follows that George Burns is the ultimate cynic, bound to Gracie by holy deadlock, I mean wedlock.

Try this exercise: Imagine that your car has just been totaled by a BMW driven by the powerful head of a major movie studio. Seize the moment to pitch some high-concept movie ideas using the law of comic opposites.

A scrooge marries a spendthrift.
A college nerd and a party beast are roommates.
A priest inherits a brothel.
A debutante takes a street punk to the prom.
A construction worker adopts a spoiled rich kid.

Another way to discover strong comic opposites is to ask of your comic character, "Who could give this person the worst possible time?" A priest is going to have more trouble with a hooker than with, say, an insurance salesman. Who would give a self-centered, arrogant football star the worst possible time? A self-centered, arrogant diva?

Obviously, not all comic opposites lead to full and complete comic stories, high-concept or otherwise. But again, notice how much easier it is to answer a simple, concrete question like "What's the comic opposite of a scrooge?" than it is to answer a broad, vague question like "What's a good idea for a movie?"

TENSION AND RELEASE

Every time you start a joke, you create some tension. The tension often develops in the form of a question: "What's this joke about?" If the joke works, then all that stored tension is released at the punchline in the form of laughter. In general, the more stored tension there is, the greater will be the comic release.

> *Last night I had this dream where I was doing stand-up comedy, and I got up and introduced myself and said, "My name is John Vorhaus, and of course that rhymes with whorehouse, and it's been that way all my life, and frankly, I'm sick of it, so now I'm changing my name."*

This is in a dream, mind you.

> *"My new name? Vordello."*

The tension in this joke is created by the awareness that the joke teller has a problem with his name, and by the underlying question of how is he going to solve that problem. The solution, which, of course, is no solution at all, releases all the stored tension. And the longer one can delay the payoff, the funnier the joke will be.

Is this true? Well, suppose I had said instead, "My name used to be Vorhaus but now it's Vordello," I might get a laugh, but it wouldn't be as big because I'd given the tension no chance to build. The mind has to contemplate the question of the joke in order to benefit from the buildup.

This is why I set that last joke in a dream, and why you see stand-up comics taking such long, roundabout routes to the point of their stories. They know how useful it is to milk the moment.

Tension and release is not only a function of time, it's often a function of circumstance as well. Any time you have an audience or a reader or a viewer concerned about you or your characters, you have a certain amount of tension stored in the form of fear. The more dire the circumstance, the greater the tension; the greater the tension, the bigger the comic relief.

There's a moment in *Butch Cassidy and the Sundance Kid* when Butch and Sundance are pinned down by a posse and trying to decide whether to jump off a cliff into the river far below. Even though their lives are on the line, they spend several minutes wrangling back and forth before Sundance announces that he flat won't jump. Butch asks him why. "I can't swim!" shouts Sundance. "You stupid fool," says Butch, "the fall will probably kill you." As the audience bursts into laughter, our heroes hurl themselves off the cliff.

Bottom line, then: To make a joke funny, delay the payoff; to make a situation funny, create dire circumstances. We'll talk more about this later as we discuss ways of raising the stakes in a comic story. For now, just think maximum tension, suspended release.

Sometimes you can get more out of a joke or a funny notion simply by saving the funny word for last. This is called *positioning the payoff.* There are three strong arguments for doing so. First, you get the most benefit from release of stored tension. Second, if the joke is truly funny, your audience will laugh at the punchline, and the rest of the line will be lost in the din. The third and most important reason for positioning the payoff at the end of the line is to make sure that all your critical setup information has been delivered. Consider this line:

> *If the universe is constantly expanding, why can't*
> *I find a place to park?*

The word that makes the joke work is "park"; it's the one that answers the question "What's this joke about?" If you phrased the joke this way, "Why can't I find a place to park, since the universe is constantly expanding?" your audience would have to wait past "park" and go all the way to the end of the line before they had enough information to get the joke. It's as if you've answered the question before asking it. And since the answer is what's funny, you squander the joke by positioning the payoff too soon.

Here are some more examples of positioning the payoff correctly.

Right: "Stop feeling sorry for yourself—you miserable loser!"

Wrong: "You miserable loser, stop feeling sorry for yourself."

The reader of the second line has to absorb the concept of "miserable loser," then read the punchline, and then go back and reconsider "miserable loser" in order to get the joke, while in the first instance, "miserable loser" is both the punchline and the key word needed to make the punchline work.

Right: "If you want to make God laugh, tell him your plans."

Wrong: "Tell God your plans if you want to make him laugh."

In this case, the tension is created by the question, "How do you make God laugh?" Turn the joke around and you give away the answer before you've posed the question.

Right: "I was voted in high school least-likely to complete the fifty-yard dash."

Wrong: "I was voted least-likely to complete the fifty-yard dash in high school."

If the words "in high school" precede the payoff, they amplify the meaning of the joke, but if they follow the payoff, they just take up space. Consider them to be inert matter, like argon gas. Purge them from your work.

Sometimes when a joke doesn't work, fixing it is just a matter of rearranging the parts. When in doubt, put the funny word last.

TELLING THE TRUTH TO COMIC EFFECT

I'm bald. I don't mind being bald. I look at it this way: I haven't combed my hair in seven years, but on the other hand, I haven't had a bad hair day, either.

This is called telling the truth to comic effect.

Johnny Carson used to do this all the time. Whenever a joke bombed, he'd make a comment or shoot the audience a look that said, in effect, "Well, that joke didn't work." Even though the joke didn't work, the truth he told behind it almost always did.

You can use this tool in almost any situation simply by stating the obvious. You could say of a two-year-old, for instance, "He has the attention span of a two-year-old." You could say to a cop who pulls you over for speeding, "I suppose I know why you stopped me." He likely won't laugh, but cops are a notoriously tough audience.

Like many cool tools, this one is reversible. Not only can you tell the truth to comic effect, you can also try

TELLING A LIE TO COMIC EFFECT

Suppose you're standing in a long line somewhere, and you say, "This sure is a long line." It's the truth, but it's not funny. Try telling a lie instead: "If this line gets any longer, they're going to assign it a zip code."

Telling a lie to comic effect is like finding the wildly inappropriate response. Simply locate the truth of a situation and then say the opposite of that. "I only want you for your mind." "Ronald Reagan was smart." "This book is worth $14.95."

These two tools work well together; if a situation doesn't call for the truth, it calls for a lie, or vice versa. As an exercise, then, stick yourself into various situations and hunt for responses that either tell the truth or tell a lie to comic effect.

Situation	Response
At the dentist's	"Novocain? No thanks."
In shark-infested waters	"Now I get my period!"

On an answering machine	"I'm kissing up to someone more important than you right now . . ."
At confession	"Trust me, faddah, you don't wanna know."
To a deaf person	" !"

Sometimes it's hard to tell whether you're telling the truth to comic effect or telling a lie to comic effect. If I stand up in front of a class and tell them that I'm worried about the Fraud Police bursting in and taking me away to fake teacher's prison, am I telling a lie or telling the truth? Obviously, I don't expect any actual cops to bust down the door, but on the other hand I am addressing a real insecurity.

In the end it doesn't matter whether you put the joke in one category or the other, or in neither category, or in both. The point of these tools is not to get all hung up on definitions but to find a reliable place to go when we need a joke and we need it now. If you invoke a tool called "telling the truth to comic effect" and it ends up producing a comic lie, I can't see that it makes a damn bit of difference. And it's my book, so I guess what I say goes.

6
TYPES OF COMIC STORIES

When you set out to tell a comic story, it's useful to know just what kind of story you're trying to tell. The rules that govern one sort of story are wildly irrelevant to another. I'm not all that hooked on the notion of following the rules (since rules, in general, are made to serve the rule makers and not you and me), but if you're writing within a genre such as comedy, you can't possibly hope to get it right unless you know what the forms and structures of that genre are. True genius works within form.

Plus there's this: Using categories is yet another way to swap a large, cluttered, unfocused creative problem for a smaller, cleaner, much more tightly organized one. Instead of asking, "What's a comic story?" or "Where's my next idea coming from?" you can ask, "What kind of comic story shall I tell?" Science tells us that the universe is moving toward increasing entropy, that is, generally speaking, from order to chaos. In knowing what sort of comic story you're telling, you fight against entropy. Isn't that comforting?

On the other hand, if you're a stand-up comic or a comic essayist or a cartoonist, this chapter may very well be, to quote the phrase, wildly irrelevant to you. If you'd like to go to study hall, I'll be happy to write you a pass. For the rest of you, skootch your chairs a little closer and we'll explore the wonderful world of comic worlds.

CENTER AND ECCENTRICS

In a center-and-eccentrics configuration, you have everyman surrounded by comic characters. The function of this everyman is to stand in for you and me, to be our eyes and ears as we visit all the kooky, wacky eccentrics of his, and our, new world.

The comic premise of a center and eccentrics story is found in the gap between our central character's normal perspective and the uncommon comic perspectives of the eccentric characters who surround him.

In the movie *Who Framed Roger Rabbit?*, Bob Hoskins is Eddie Valiant, an average guy lost in a world of cartoon characters. Roger, Jessica, Mr. Acme, Judge Doom, and the weasels all conspire to give Eddie the worst possible time. We, the audience, see the comedy of this world through Eddie's bemused and long-suffering eyes.

In *Monty Python's Life of Brian*, poor Brian gets chased and harassed and abused by one comic character after another until he finally ends up hanging from a cross, dying horribly while cheery people around him sing, "Always look on the bright side of life."

Television loves center and eccentrics. Bob Newhart's shows have always used this structure, as did *Barney Miller* and everything Judd Hirsch ever did. In *Taxi*, Hirsch, our everyman, was surrounded by a punch-drunk boxer, an acid casualty, a corrupt little man, and a foreigner. Episodes of that show routinely milked the gap between the way Hirsch's Alex Rieger viewed the world and the way it was viewed by Tony, Jim, Louie, and Latka in turn. Week in and week out on *The Mary Tyler Moore Show*, we would see everygal Mary pitted against Ted's ego, Lou's gruff exterior, Murray's nebbishness, Rhoda's *kvetching*, etc.

Is *Catch-22* center and eccentrics? Only if you don't consider Yossarian to be eccentric in his own right. Certainly he keeps telling everyone he's not crazy, but who'd believe a crazy man like that? Columnist Art Buchwald doesn't have an eccentric point of view per se; rather, he assigns quirky outlooks to the endless parade of fictional acquaintances and friends about whom he writes.

The point of identifying center and eccentrics is not so that you'll know it when you see it, in a self-referential "Where's Waldo?" kind of way (though, in fact, isn't Waldo the ultimate center among eccentrics?). The point is to help you build your own strong comic stories, and center and eccentrics is nicely suited to the task.

As you try the following exercise, recognize that the amount of actual writing you'll be doing is about to go way up. Until now, we've traded mostly in lists and lines. For some time to come, we'll be writing whole paragraphs of comic stuff, so if you've been scrawling in the margins or on the back of your hand, now would be a good time to move to the computer or get that notebook going in earnest.

Here's the task: Name a central character and assign him or her a normal, non-comic perspective. Next, stick him in a situation, the place where he works or lives, for example. Now create about half a dozen other characters, and invest them all with strong comic perspectives. As you do this exercise, keep words to a minimum; if you can't define a character in one sentence, I don't think you can define him at all. As I do this exercise, I find that I've created a situation comedy called *We're In This Together*.

> SALLY CROWDER is the long-suffering mom of identical teen triplets. CHIP has made his life a shrine to Elle MacPherson. SKIP should have "Born to ace physics" tattooed on his arm. SCOOTER would sell the cat if the price was right. Sally's husband is GEORGE, he of the Teflon-coated brain pan, and the next door neighbor, MRS. BRICKLE, thinks there's no problem so large or complicated that it can't be cured with fudge.

What I hope you'll discover is that it's far easier to springboard into a story with a point of departure like this than with, say, "A guy goes to work in a zoo." What beginning comic writers, especially in situation comedy, often fail to realize is that a comic story is not about a setting or a situation or a predicament, but about strong and enduring lines of conflict between and among the characters. Center and eccentrics tells you immediately who your hero is, who he's up against, and where his lines of conflict lie.

FISH OUT OF WATER

In a fish-out-of-water tale, we find either a normal character in a comic world or a comic character in a normal world. You, clever reader, will immediately recognize this configuration as clash of context played out story-wide. You will also notice that fish-out-of-water resembles center and eccentrics, because it often involves plonking a character down spang-blam in the midst of some very strange creatures indeed. Right and right again. That's fine. Remember what we said about pigeonholes and squished pigeons—categories are made to be broken.

Virtually every time-travel story features a normal character in a comic world. *Back to the Future, Time Bandits, Sleeper,* etc., present us with the clashing comic perspectives of the present versus the future or the present versus the past. To build a story on this structure, simply take a typical dude and put him in a far-away place, either literally or metaphorically.

Turn this structure around and you have a comic character in a normal world. Most space-alien comedies fall into this category for reasons that are self-evident. *Mork and Mindy, E.T., My Step-mother Is an Alien, My Favorite Martian,* and *ALF* all find their humor in the gap between the comic character's comic perspective and the conventional reality (our reality) that now surrounds him. *Trading Places* and *The Prince and the Pauper* each feature two characters in one another's world. Of course, for the ultimate fish-out-of-water tale, look no further than *Splash* or *The Little Mermaid.*

Recognize that fish-out-of-water stories don't require an actual physical change of place. Often a character undergoes an internal change, and that's what sets the story in motion. In *Big,* the Tom Hanks character goes from being a child to an adult. That's what throws this fish out of his water. Likewise in *Tootsie*: Michael Dorsey gets into drag, which kicks his tale into gear. And then, just to close this circle, put Tom Hanks in drag and you have the short-lived situation comedy *Bosom Buddies.*

I must tell you that fish-out-of-water is an open invitation to splitting hairs. Is *Northern Exposure* about a normal character in a comic world or a comic character in a normal world? From Joel Fleischman's perspective, the answer is the former, but from the perspective of the residents of Cecily, it's the other way around. Likewise in *Sister Act,* who's the comic character, Whoopi Goldberg or all those nutty nuns? Both. Neither. It couldn't matter less. All that matters is that you get a feel for taking someone and sticking him someplace he doesn't belong— and the more he doesn't belong, the better.

What we're really after here is putting our heroes through hell. We want them in worlds that will give them the worst possible time. I've always shied away from this kind of thinking, because basically I'm a nice guy and I want nice things to happen to my friends. But these are comic characters, not friends, and in order to make their story funny you really have to put them in hot water. Once you learn to take sick and twisted pleasure in making their lives miserable, your stories will become much more interesting and funny. Apply exaggeration to fish out of water, and soon you won't just have a fish out of water, you'll have a dying and desperate fish flopping around on the beach writhing and gasping for breath. Fun!

It may be useful to boil down some familiar fish-out-of-water stories to one-sentence tellings of their tales. I'll try a few, and you do a few on your own.

> A man who wants desperately to leave his old life behind ends up stuck in a small town reliving the same day over and over again. (*Groundhog Day*)

> A timid romance novelist finds herself on a quest for treasure in a South American jungle. (*Romancing the Stone*)

> An upwardly mobile black family moves into privilege on the Upper East Side. (*The Jeffersons*)

> A stop-at-nothing businesswoman gets saddled with a baby. (*Baby Boom*)

> An ordinary man awakens from a night of fitful dreams to discover that he's been turned into a giant cockroach. (Kafka's *Metamorphosis*)

Metamorphosis?!? Okay, so it's not a laugh riot. Still, it's an authentic fish-out-of-water tale, and drama, after all, is just comedy without the laughs. Also, notice how these characters' new

worlds are, in some sense, comic opposites of the characters themselves. The woman who wants a baby least is the one who gets
one. The woman who fears adventure stumbles into one. This is
the sort of dynamic conflict you want.

Okay, next exercise: write some one-line ideas for fish-out-
of-water stories. Try to give them titles as well.

> A Martian wins a trip to Earth on a game show and winds
> up in the Old West masquerading as an Indian. (*Cowboys
> and Aliens*)

> A nun who doubts her vocation ends up running a casino.
> (*Queen of Clubs*)

> A downtrodden housewife changes places with Joan of
> Arc. (*Saint Jane*)

> A wicked old man dies and gets sent to heaven by mis-
> take. (*Heaven is Hell*)

Again, not all of our ideas will be keepers. That's okay; we
know by now that they don't have to be. With fish out of water,
you often have to throw back the little ones.

CHARACTER COMEDY

Character comedy is direct emotional war between strong comic
opposites. If you want to build an enduring situation comedy, or
a strong comic film, or a short story, or a stage routine, or even a
comic strip, you can do far worse than to invoke the law of comic
opposites on the level of your premise. It's a natural law; there is
no right of appeal.

Calvin and Hobbes, in the eponymous comic strip of the same

name, wage constant war for control. It's the same kind of war waged between Ralph Kramden and Ed Norton in *The Honeymooners*, between Wodehouse's Bertie and Jeeves, between the Bill Murray character and the Richard Dreyfuss character in *What About Bob?*, it's the war fought in *Love and War* and *Chico and the Man*, and in about a zillion other stories I'm sure you can also name.

Character comedy is often character romance as well, so that the direct emotional war is waged between haters who will become lovers in the end. Sam and Diane on *Cheers*, Dave and Maddie in *Moonlighting*, Tracy and Hepburn in everything; the partners in these pairings are designed to give each other hell. Be certain that if they were any less annoying to each other, they'd be a good deal less funny to us.

To make a character comedy work, you need strong forces driving a couple apart, and equally strong forces holding them together. In *All in the Family*, Archie and Meathead are related by marriage. In *48 Hours*, Nick Nolte and Eddie Murphy each have life-and-death reasons to stick together and solve the crime, plus a ticking clock to beat. On *Cheers*, Sam and Diane hate each other, but their sexual chemistry binds them with the power of endocrine superglue. This is a good thing.

Character comedy doesn't always require diametric comic opposites to work. In *K-9*, Jim Belushi is a cop partnered with a dog. In *Stop or My Mom Will Shoot*, Sylvester Stallone is a cop partnered with his mom. In *Cop and a Half*, Burt Reynolds is a cop partnered with a kid. In each of these cases, the hero's nemesis is not so much his opposite as his catalyst for misery.

Catalyst for misery. That's a useful phrase to contemplate as you do the next exercise. Try to build your stories around characters who can be one another's true catalyst for misery. Don't be afraid to be mean. These people are figments of your imagination; you can torment them all you like.

Also notice that as we move further from list-making to storytelling, you will be hugely tempted to get caught up in the details of each new story. Resist that urge. At this point, it's not necessary to know any more about your story than the single sentence that spells it out. In the next chapter, I'll outline a shorthand for "growing" your story to the next level. For now, though, let's just keep flexing our comic muscles and see what we get.

A conservative C.E.O. takes his radical son into the family business.

A straight woman and a gay man compete for the same guy.

An electrician and a magician team up to save the world.

A doctor marries a hypochondriac.

A cop gets partnered with a rock star.

A lady lawyer defends her con artist ex-husband in a murder case.

Don't worry if all your pairings don't seem to fit neatly into this category. As we've already discovered, the best comic stories cross boundaries. Is *Northern Exposure* center and eccentrics, or fish-out-of-water, or character comedy? Answer: D, all of the above. In fact, the best thing to do with an idea that you particularly like is see how many different types of stories you can tell with the same concept. This will add depth and texture to your comic ideas. So now let's add magic into the mix.

POWERS

In a comic story built around magical powers, the comic premise is the power itself. The gap between real reality and comic reality is the presumed existence of some magic or some fantasy element. You may remember an old television show called *My Mother the Car*, in which the central conceit was that a man's mother could come back and make trouble for him by living in his 1928 Porter. If you bought the premise, you bought the show; if not, you watched *Combat* or *Rawhide* or something on public television. In the same era, you might have watched *Bewitched* or *I Dream of Jeannie* or *Mr. Ed* or *My Favorite Martian* or *The Flying Nun*. Some have called this era the golden age of TV magic. Actually, no one's called it that but me, and now you may too, if you wish.

Alien adventures, as we have already discussed, are almost always fish-out-of-water tales. They're also, by definition, powers tales, the "magic" of extra-terrestrial life on earth. Other science-fantasy stories are "powers" stories as well. Examples include *Honey, I Shrunk the Kids, Honey, I Blew Up the Kid, Honey, I Shipped the Kids to Cleveland*, what have you. As Arthur C. Clarke said, "Magic is just advanced technology."

Readers and viewers have a tremendous tolerance for magic in their comic stories. This is called their "willing suspension of disbelief." You establish the rules of your world, ask that your audience take those rules as given, and proceed from there. If the audience knows going in, for example, that this is a story about an invisible man, they'll tolerate almost any stupid explanation of how that invisibility happened. Stealth technology? Accidental exposure to radiation? Pickled cloves of garlic? They won't care! If the story is interesting and funny, they really won't give a damn whether the explanation makes sense or not. They're along for the ride.

But once you have them on the ride, you can't change the rules in the middle. If you write a ghost story where your ghosts can walk through walls in the first scene but can't at the climax, your audience will get a headache and go out for popcorn. They may even slip over to the next screen in the multiplex, where *New Glorx in Town* is playing to rave reviews. At least in that picture, a Glorx behaves the way a Glorx is supposed to behave.

So if you're interested in building a comic story on magical powers, keep these two thoughts in mind: Use one simple premise to get your story going ("witches exist" or "people can change bodies") and then be consistent in the way your characters use their magic.

A fat man and a thin man change bodies.

The world is threatened by a race of hyper-intelligent wombats.

James Joyce is reincarnated as a game show host.

A woman marries a robot.

A boy and his dog change places.

A mime is entertaining.

I mostly used clash of context and exaggeration to find my magic and put it into play. Also, notice how fine the focus is. I'm only after one piece of information: What's a story about powers? It's always easier to find things when you have fewer places to look. Try finding some of that magic now.

Powers stories are not my personal favorites because they don't usually lead to deep emotional conflict. I'm sorry, but a talking dog will only carry you so far. But magic does have its place. Just make sure that your magical power is a new and fascinating one, and then be true to your rules. After that, it's easy. Just twitch your nose, blink your eyes, or wiggle your little finger . . .

ENSEMBLE COMEDY

In an ensemble comedy, we have a group of people in conflict with each other and with the world. While it's possible to identify one main character or hero within the group, the best ensemble comedies dispense with this distinction and engage our interest in all the characters more or less equally. These stories are often "human" comedies, because the presence of this so-called "group protagonist" easily opens the door to discussion of real emotional issues within and among members of the group.

Examples of ensemble comedies in film include *The Big Chill*, *M*A*S*H*, *The Return of the Secaucus Seven*, *Peter's Friends*, *This is Spinal Tap*, and *Indian Summer*. On television, we find *Cheers*, *Murphy Brown*, and *The Golden Girls*. In the funny pages, there's *Doonesbury* and *For Better or Worse*. The key to an ensemble comedy is the group's commonly held goal or enemy. *Cheers* is a character conflict when it's Sam versus Diane but an ensemble comedy when the whole *Cheers* crew takes on an unruly customer or a con artist or the crosstown rival bar. Likewise in *M*A*S*H*, there's clear character conflict between Hawkeye and Major Burns or Hawkeye and Hot Lips, but when wounded soldiers arrive, the group unites to serve their common goal. In *The Golden Girls*, the group protagonist struggles against aging. In *For Better or Worse*, the family struggles to understand what being a family means.

The trick to making an ensemble comedy work is to layer in sufficient lines of conflict *within* the group to make the story worth watching. It's not enough to have a bunch of scientists battling a Japanese monster—you want them at each other's throats as well.

This is a particularly tough nut to crack. You need a whole slate of strong comic characters, each imbued with strong, and divergent, comic perspectives. You have to drive them apart with their differences, and yet link them to an overriding common goal or struggle. Draw your characters too broadly and you end up with a cartoon like *Gilligan's Island*, where all the conflict is global conflict, and nothing is at stake except how will Gilligan keep them trapped on the island this week? If your characters are too strident, you kill all their fun. Sure, the people in *Poseidon Adventure* have a common goal, but are they funny? Well, yes, but only by accident.

An ensemble comedy is kind of a meta-story, borrowing from character comedy, clash of context, fish-out-of-water, and powers, and whipping all these diverse elements together in a dynamic, organic stew. Because it relies so heavily on authentic comic characters, it's just about the hardest type of comic story to write. Nevertheless, we shall try.

A group of Irish schoolboys make life hell for their headmaster and for each other.

After their mother and father are killed in a car accident, seven sisters try to make it as a family.

A bunch of hackers get trapped inside a computer.

A gang of misfits take a second-rate rugby team to a national championship.

An Indian tribe occupies a New York City skyscraper in an effort to win back Manhattan.

An art forgery ring is haunted by the ghost of Vincent van Gogh.

The Mormon Tabernacle Choir gets transported back in time and must sing its way off Devil's Island.

It's not enough to have a great premise for an ensemble comedy. You must also be prepared to do the hard work of treating each of your characters as the hero of his or her own story, and create strong, compelling stories for everyone. Then you must figure out how to interleave these stories to create an interesting and intricate total tale. No one said it was easy. On the other hand, if it's easy you want, I commend your attention to . . .

SLAPSTICK

Slapstick comedy is just about the easiest sort of comedy to get right because, as Gertrude Stein once said of Oakland, California, "There is no *there* there." With slapstick, you don't have to worry about inner conflict or emotional core issues or any of the things that make all writing, and comic writing in particular, really brutally hard. All you have to do is make it funny in a very superficial way.

Easy as slipping on a banana peel.

A slapstick character never experiences self-doubt. In *Gilligan's Island*, Gilligan may feel bad about breaking the radio, or sleepwalking through the Professor's satellite dish, or scaring off the Russian cosmonaut, but he never questions his essential "Gilliganness." In his own mind, he's always okay. In a slapstick story or a slapstick moment, then, the comic premise is the gap between the slapstick character's self-assurance and his manifest incompetence.

Look at Lucy. The classic episodes of *I Love Lucy* always find Lucy trying to prove herself capable in a situation that invariably proves the opposite. One week she's trying to squeeze into a dancer's costume that is three sizes too small. The next week she's on the camping trip from hell. But nothing that happens to Lucy can ever shake her essential core of confidence.

This thread of rock-ribbed self-confidence runs throughout all the slapstick greats: Peter Sellers' Inspector Clouseau never ever doubts his ability to solve the crime. Dagwood Bumstead takes great pride in his napping and his big sandwiches and his other bad habits. Jerry Lewis may be an inveterate bumbler, but *not in his own mind.*

Because slapstick comedy denies self-doubt, slapstick comedy is physical comedy as opposed to cerebral comedy. That's why you find slapstick in television and film and on stage and in the Sunday funnies, but not in fiction or comic commentary. (The word s*lapstick*, by the way, comes from a tool of the same name, used in vaudeville and elsewhere; it made a loud slapping sound when used by one actor to strike another. An amazing factoid to share with your friends.)

Slapstick comedy is abuse comedy, but what makes it work is the audience's awareness that the target of abuse is getting exactly what he deserves. A pie in the face is funniest if the face belongs to a pompous jerk. To create slapstick comedy, then, start by creating comic characters with delusions of grandeur. Then put these characters in situations designed to torment those delusions.

An arrogant English professor is made to coach a working-class soccer team.

A decathalete suddenly can't control his feet.

A crazy old cat lover inherits a dozen puppies.

A white-collar criminal does time in a maximum security prison.

A cagey gambler hits the world's worst streak of bad luck.

A spoiled yuppie is cast away on a desert island.

You'll no doubt notice some similarity between your slapstick story ideas and those from other categories, notably character conflict and fish-out-of-water. Whether these stories ultimately become slapstick or not depends largely on your treatment of the central characters. If you construct a comic character with no sense of self, and no self-doubt, he or she almost can't help but become a "tall poppy," the sort of character we want to see cut down.

Of course, it's possible to aim your metaphorical pie-in-the-face at someone or something entirely outside of the story you've set out to tell. In this case, you've entered the world of . . .

SATIRE AND PARODY

Satire attacks the substance of a social or cultural icon or phenomenon. Parody attacks the style of an art form. Vaughan Meader's *The First Family* satirized President John F. Kennedy, while Mel Brook's *Spaceballs* parodied space-adventure movies. *Airplane* parodied disaster movies. *You Can't Take It With You* satirized rationalism. *This is Spinal Tap* parodied rockumentaries. *In Living*

Color parodies other television shows and films, but also satirizes racism, sexism, etc. Political cartoonists are satirists. The Rutles parodied the Beatles. The Capitol Steps satirize politics.

The common denominator between satire and parody is this: Both find their comic premise in the gap between the world as they present it and the world as their audience understands it to be. This requires the audience to step outside the show it's watching in order to get the joke.

If Dana Carvey is doing his George Bush impression, for example, viewers will only find it funny if they have an understanding of how the real George Bush normally talks and acts. Likewise, a parody of horror movies will be lost on someone who's never actually seen a horror film.

Parody and satire, then, become a tricky business because you have to gauge accurately how much your audience knows about your target. You might find it hilariously funny to mock the rules of the Malaysian legislature, but if your audience knows nothing of Malaysian politics, the point, and the joke, will be lost. To recall our class clown and class nerd again, the class clown parodies the teacher, while the class nerd parodies a book that no one else has bothered to read.

Another danger of parody and satire is that they only work when the viewer steps outside the story or the reader leaves the page. Whenever this happens, you run the risk that they might not bother to return. For instance, if you're writing an otherwise self-contained comic story and suddenly throw in a reference to Mahatma Gandhi, it may be hilariously funny and yet still not work for you. Your reader has to stop and remember everything he knows about Gandhi, "call up his file," so to speak, and then measure that information against the reference you've just made. Even if he gets the joke, you've broken up your narrative flow, taken the reader off the page. Unless the joke is a damned good one, you stand to lose more than you gain.

The best parody and satire operate on two levels at the same time. You might have a fish-out-of-water tale that involves a comic character in a new and challenging world and yet, at the same time, mocks a facet of the world with which we're quite familiar. The joke takes the reader off the page, but the strong, compelling story brings him back. *The Bullwinkle Show* always did this very well. On one level, it was a cartoon, showing the resourceful Rocky and the dim-bulb Bullwinkle in dire and comic circumstances. The kids loved it. On another level, the show was a dense allusional puzzle, full of delights and surprises for adults: "Oh, Boris Badenov, the bad guy; oh, Boris Godunov, the Russian tsar; oh, bad enough/good enough; I get it. Ha!"

The key to making your parodies and satires work, then, is to make sure that your target is well understood by your audience and that your framing story works on some other level as well. Also remember to use your tool of exaggeration. Parody and satire require a huge gap between your story and your target.

> A studio executive tries to turn her talentless pretty-boy lover into a star.
>
> An idiot savant becomes a Wall Street stock mogul.
>
> Misguided entrepreneurs open a theme park based on the works of Marcel Proust.
>
> A Glorxian immigrant in pursuit of the American Dream takes over a McDonald's franchise.

Notice that each of the above satires has a clearly defined target chosen from the real world.

> A deaf-mute hosts a talk show.
>
> A porno movie earns a G-rating.
>
> A jugband plays Wagner's *Ring* cycle.
>
> Senior citizens star in a teen comedy.
>
> The life of Buddha is done as a musical.

In parody, it's necessary for the parody to be the same in form and structure as the thing it parodies. My last example, *Oh, Buddha!*, would have the same shape and self-serious tone as *Jesus Christ, Superstar.* Try some now.

SATIRE:

PARODY:

Notice that if you did all the exercises in this chapter, you now have a working vocabulary of fifty, sixty, seventy different starting points for comic stories. It took no magic to find these stories, no outrageous creative gifts. All we did was swap the large question, "What's a comic story?" for smaller questions, "What are examples of *this particular kind* of comic story." I hope that you're becoming much more confident in your comic abilities, now seeing them to be rooted in logical process and simple, straightforward creative problem-solving.

7

THE COMIC THROUGHLINE

What's a throughline? My dictionary doesn't list the word and silently accuses me of making it up. Well let's just call a throughline a simple, direct path from the start to the end of a tale. If the tale is a comic one, then the throughline is a Comic Throughline, a phrase I've trademarked so that when Comic Throughline sportswear and coffee mugs and Comic Throughline action figures come on the market, I can really cash in.

Not all forms of comedy involve story, although if you look hard enough, you can find the beginning, middle and end of any comic moment, even a joke, even a pratfall, even the launch, flight, and impact of the lowly pie in the face. Nor is all storytelling comic, although if you look hard enough at this throughline thing, I think you'll discover that it works equally well with serious stories as with comic.

In fact, I know it does because I've used it myself for dramatic stories, and will probably call it (and trademark it as) the Dramatic Throughline in another book some day. You'll notice in this chapter that I draw examples from comic and dramatic stories alike and don't draw much distinction between the two. To my mind, the difference between comedy and drama is a matter of exaggeration, perspective, inappropriate responses, and the wide gap of the comic premise. But these are differences of tone, not structure. About the only place that comic structure veers away from dramatic structure is in the matter of endings, a matter we'll discuss, well, at the end.

I could go into a whole big thing about how structure is structure is structure, but let's just leave it at this: Whether your story is comic or serious, it has to work first as a *story*. This chapter offers a template for making that difficult thing happen.

Some people might try to tell you that a comic story doesn't require structure. "It's just comedy," they'll say, "all that matters are the jokes." Trust me, those people are wrong and soon will try to sell you dubious propositions in real estate or Michael Bolton CDs. A well-structured story gives jokes a place to happen. It tells the audience whose story to follow. If they don't know who to follow, they don't know who to care about. If they don't care, they don't laugh.

So while we're going to spend this chapter talking about something other than comedy, in the strictest sense of the word, please suspend your disbelief and imagine that we're developing something in fact crucial to comedy. Your money cheerfully retained if not completely satisfied.

I think that cracking the story is just about the hardest part of a comic writer's job. One reason for this is that what makes us funny—a knack for comic invention—doesn't necessarily help us cope with the rigors and disciplines of storytelling. Another reason (I'm sure you won't be shocked to hear) is *lack of proper tools*.

In my time, I've haunted bookstores where you can't swing a dead cat without hitting a rack of massive tomes on story structure and scriptwriting and screenwriting: *Zen in the Art of the Plot Pivot*, *Act Two Made E-Z*, what have you. I've found almost all such books to be almost incomprehensibly dense. It's not that they don't work; it's just that they didn't work for me. I'm a simple guy. I needed a simpler system.

So I built my own. What I wanted was a way of writing the barest bones of my story in ten sentences or less, so that I could discover with a minimum of work whether I had an interesting, whole and solid story or not. What I came up with was this:

> Who is the hero?
> What does the hero want?
> The door opens.
> The hero takes control.
> A monkey wrench is thrown.
> Things fall apart.

The hero hits bottom.
The hero risks all.
What does the hero get?

Up till now in this book, we've only developed stories to the level of a sentence or two. With this structure, we'll move to the next level—a paragraph or two—where, if all goes according to plan, you'll be able to see simply and clearly the beginning, middle and end of your tale, plus some vital stops along the way.

The Comic Throughline won't give you all the answers. It won't tell you how Aunt Celia could have robbed the bank in Cleveland if she was in Hawaii with Señor Guernevaca at the time. I have some strategies for solving that sort of story problem, but they come later. For now, we just want to know if our story is complete and authentic. With a minimum of work.

Which is not to say that the tool doesn't take practice. It will definitely seem clunky and awkward, more paint-by-numbers or fill-in-the-blanks than genuine comic story development. After a few times through, though, the tool will become comfortable in your hand. And then, interestingly enough, it will disappear from view. Soon you'll use it just to check your work, to make sure your story is tracking correctly (not like subtracting to check your addition, which only proves that you can make the same mistake twice.) Ultimately, if it works for you as it works for me, it will illuminate a part of your storytelling map that may previously have only been marked, "This space intentionally left blank."

Well that's the plan, anyhow. Let's throw it out the window and see if it lands.

WHO IS THE HERO?

Every story is about someone. It can be several someones, as in *The Big Chill*, or about someone who becomes a some*thing*, as in *Metamorphosis*, or about something who never was a someone, as in *The Bear*. Until you decide who your story is about, you have no hope of discovering *what* your story is about. Imagine a private detective who tried to tail a suspect without first deciding which suspect to tail. Can't be done.

The first order of business, then, is to select your hero. At this point, don't take "hero" to mean some sort of larger-than-life ad-venturer like Conan or Roseanne Arnold. Smaller-than-life adven-turers, like Yossarian and Woody Allen, make excellent heroes, too. By hero we simply mean the protagonist, the main character, the star of the literal or figurative show. For the purposes of this ex-ercise, any hero will do, though if you're going to develop a comic story, you need to start with a strong comic character as outlined in chapter four. Also, please remember that while I use the per-sonal pronoun "he" for convenience, I am in no way suggesting that your hero should be male. It's just a limitation of the language.

Film heroes include Sylvester Stallone in *Rocky*, Scarlett O'Hara in *Gone With the Wind*, Luke Skywalker in *Star Wars*, Dorothy in *The Wizard of Oz*, E.T. in *E.T.*, and the courageous Japanese jour-nalist who fought Godzilla to a draw. Television sitcom heroes include Archie Bunker, Rob Petrie, Gilligan, Seinfeld, and poor, long-suffering Oliver Douglas. Heroes in fiction include Anne of Green Gables, Sissy Hankshaw, Tom Sawyer, Rip van Winkle, and Bartleby the Scrivener.

Interestingly, each of us is the hero of his or her own adven-ture. You're the hero of your story, I'm the hero of mine. Mao Zedong was the hero of the Long March. Jesus Christ starred in the Gospels.

Can a story have two heroes? Sure: Woodward and Bernstein, Butch and Sundance, Gertrude Stein and Alice B. Toklas. The problem is that each of these characters is the hero of his or her own story, and to understand their stories completely, you'll even-tually have to separate them and track them individually. You'll save yourself a lot of grief, at least in this chapter, if you declare your hero to be a single individual and develop the story through him.

So what I'd like you to do now is create a character to run through this throughline with me as the chapter progresses. Build someone new from the comic perspective up or use a character you've invented in an earlier exercise. You can even look at your neighbor's paper. The proctors have left the room.

My hero, then, is ALBERT COLLIER, a young dreamer in 1915. His strong comic perspective is *curiosity*: he's a tinkerer driven to invention. His flaws include gawkiness, curiosity, sexual inno-cence, intellectual arrogance, painful shyness, impulsiveness, and fear of heights. His humanity includes intelligence, compassion, creativity, a sense of humor, good looks, charm, and a strong desire to change the world with his inventions. We see exaggeration in Albert's awful bumbling clumsiness, in his tendency to take things apart that he can't put back together, in his sexual innocence—a lady's naked ankle makes him blush—and in the wildly inventive but spectacularly unsuccessful things he builds. In short, Albert Collier is a young man who's really going places—if only he can stay out of his own way.

Take a moment now to invent your hero and describe him or her on paper. Limit yourself to a paragraph of detail, and then boil all that detail back down to one sentence. Don't stop until you can identify your hero in one sentence, for that's your strong clue that he's become clear to you. At the same time, don't get hung up on "right" answers. Every character is subject to massive change without notice, and while it's true that you can't discover your story until you've discovered your hero, it's also true that your story will reveal things about your hero that neither of you ever knew.

WHAT DOES THE HERO WANT?

Once we've identified the hero of our tale, we next have to know what he wants: What's his goal, strong desire, or need? It turns out that an interesting and well-constructed comic hero has not one strong need but two: his *outer need* and his *inner need*. Put simply, the outer need is what the hero thinks he wants and his inner need is what he really wants.

For instance, your hero may think that he wants to build a successful business when what he really wants is to retire to the woods and paint. Or he may think that he wants to join the Navy, but what he really wants is to get his darn father off his back. Or he may think that he wants his dead wife back, but what he really wants is to come to terms with her death. Again, you may not see such dark psychology as grist for the old humor mill, but I think you'll find that it is.

In *Even Cowgirls Get the Blues*, Sissy Hankshaw's outer need is to hitchhike, but her inner need is to find her place in the world. In *Tootsie*, Michael Dorsey's outer need is to get work as an actor, but his inner need is to discover his true self. In *City Slickers*, Billy Crystal's outer need is to have a raw adventure, but his inner need is to have an authentic life experience. In *Pretty in Pink*, Molly Ringwald's outer need is to prove herself to the snobs at school, but her inner need is to prove herself to herself.

Sitcom characters have outer and inner needs as well. Mary Richards' outer need is to take care of her friends, but her inner need is to stand up for herself. Archie Bunker's outer need is to validate his bigoted view of the world, but his inner need is to understand a difficult world. Murphy Brown's outer need is to prove herself to everyone, but her inner need is to prove herself to herself.

In the New Testament, Jesus's outer need is to help the poor, but his inner need is to know God. I won't speculate on Mao's inner need on the Long March. Possibly to keep his feet warm. What are your outer need and inner need? The answer to this question won't necessarily help your comic storytelling, but it's interesting to ponder just the same. Consider it extra credit.

Here are some more examples, just to make sure we're all tracking the same target. In *When Harry Met Sally*, Harry's outer need is to prove he's right, but his inner need is to find love. In *Romancing the Stone*, Joan Wilder's outer need is to save her sister, but her inner need is to find love. In *Groundhog Day*, the Bill Murray character's outer need is to get out of his dead-end life, but his inner need is to find love.

We see this over and over again in comic movies: No matter what the hero thinks he wants, what he really wants is love. It may even be that the presence or absence of love as an issue is the difference between a comic and a dramatic story. I decline to speculate, for that's the stuff of doctoral dissertations, not pop "how-to" tomes. Suffice it to say that if you can't find any other inner need for your character, assign the need for love. You won't go too far wrong.

But don't get fooled by the word "love" any more than by the word "hero." There are all sorts of love besides romantic love. Billy Crystal loves that calf in *City Slickers*, but doesn't want to marry it (as far as we can tell). Steve Martin loves his daughter in *Father of the Bride*. Luke Skywalker loves the rebel alliance in *Star Wars*.

Can a hero have more than one inner need and outer need? Sure, why the heck not? In *Romancing the Stone*, Joan Wilder needs romance, and adventure, and to save her sister's life. In *Star Wars*, Luke Skywalker needs his manhood, adventure, and love. He has to defeat Darth Vader and to save the rebel alliance and to master the Force. Busy guy. Just as the most interesting stories have many levels of conflict, so the most interesting heroes have many levels of comic need. On the other hand, two are sufficient, so long as the inner need and outer need are real. So think about your character for a moment and assign those needs to him now.

In my story about Albert Collier (working title *Everybody's Dream Come True*), Albert's outer need is to invent one damn thing that works, but his inner need is to become a man.

I don't worry that Albert's inner need—the need to come of age—has been explored before. Such needs are universal; they're what make a story worth telling. Don't worry that your hero's need is already "taken." When you dress it up in detail, you'll make it uniquely your own.

Also don't worry if your hero's needs change later. Right now, all we want to do is set the story in motion. A story is a dynamic thing. Nothing's set in stone until the type is set in print. So feel free to be reckless and bold in your choices. After all, you can't go back and fix a broken story until you've broken it pretty good in the first place.

Oh, and I'd just like to say that it's not enough to think about these things. You really need to write them down. You are? Oh, good. Well, I won't mention it again.

THE DOOR OPENS

Now that we've established our hero's strong outer need and inner need, we need to kick his story into gear. What we want is to thrust him into some new and challenging world, a place away from home, literally or figuratively, where he gets a chance to go for the thing he thinks he needs. If Dorothy in *The Wizard of Oz* thinks she wants to leave home (she really wants to *accept* home), the door opens when the tornado comes and takes her away.

In a fish-out-of-water tale, the fish leaves his pond. In a character comedy, the comic opposites meet. In a powers tale, your hero finds the magic. On the page, so far, your story might look something like this:

> PAULA PILDUSKI is a prim 'n' proper bride-to-be. Her strong outer need is to get home in time to marry BILL. Her strong inner need is to discover that she's marrying the wrong man before it's too late. The door opens when she arranges to ride home with ANDREW FERGUSON, anarchist of the soul and, unbeknownst to Paula, her ultimate Mr. Right.

In *Weird Science*, two teenage nerdnoes have the strong outer need to be *popular*. The door opens when computer magic creates the girl of their dreams. In *Play It Again Sam*, Woody Allen wants to succeed with women. The door opens when Humphrey Bogart comes alive for him. In *Even Cowgirls Get the Blues*, Sissy Hankshaw wants to hitchhike. The door opens when she becomes old enough to hit the road. In *The Big Chill*, a group of college pals have the strong comic need to come to terms with their past. The door opens when the suicide of a peer brings them all back together again.

An episode of *The Mary Tyler Moore Show* might start with Mary's strong outer need to have Ted and Lou be better friends. The door opens when they agree to try. An episode of *All in the Family* might start with Archie's strong outer need to prove that liberals lack the courage of their convictions. The door opens when Michael refuses to back a student strike. In the sitcom *Love Will Find a Way* (don't see newspaper for local listings—I just made it up), the hero is Walter, a young widower, whose strong outer need is to find a mother for his kids. The door opens when he hires a lady chauffeur.

Now you know and I know that Walter and the chauffeur will become lovers in the end. Thus, in a situation comedy, the hero's strong outer need can drive an episode and/or an entire series. Murphy Brown's strong outer need to prove herself to others leads her to take a job at FYI in the wake of her stint at the Betty Ford Center. Dobie Gillis's strong outer need to find the girl of his dreams is the engine that motors his show.

As an exercise, try creating a couple of new situation comedies by starting with their central character's strong outer need. For example . . .

> In *Flappers!*, our hero's strong outer need to be in show business drives him to buy and renovate a derelict burlesque house.

> In *Rising Starr*, a young boy with a strong need for control in his world finds a magic meteor that gives him the power to make wishes come true.

> In *Home of the Brave*, a newlywed couple's dream of owning their own home leads them to buy a haunted house.

In *A Fish Called Wanda*, John Cleese's Reggie has the strong need to free himself from his dull, conservative life. The door opens when he meets Wanda. Wanda, on the other hand, has the strong need to recover stolen diamonds, and the door opens when she meets Reggie, who can help her do it. You can see from this example that each of your lead characters can be treated as the hero of his or her own story. In *The Prince and the Pauper*, both of the main characters have a need to reinvent themselves, and the door opens for each when he meets the other.

In *Risky Business*, Tom Cruise wants a taste of independence. The door opens when his parents go away on vacation. In *Home Alone*, Macaulay Culkin wants everyone to leave him the heck alone. The door opens when his whole family goes away on vacation.

From the hero's point of view, the opening door is either a problem or an opportunity, a threat or a welcoming hand. In murder mysteries, the door opens with the discovery of a corpse. In quest adventures, like *Lord of the Rings*, the opening door is the call to the quest. The common denominator is this: The opening door *upsets the applecart*. From the moment the door opens, things for your hero can never be the same.

Or, to put it another way, the opening door makes your hero an offer he can't refuse. So make your opening door as compelling or as dire you can. Then yank your hero through it.

Another way to open the door is to offer your hero something he really wants but maybe can't handle. Cinderella wants to go to the ball, but when she gets there, she has to be up to the challenge of winning Prince Charming.

On the other hand, the opening door can look like your hero's worst nightmare come true. In *Baby Boom*, Diane Keaton plays a selfish yuppie on a high-powered career track. Her opening door—she inherits a baby—is the last thing she thinks she wants. Of course, in terms of her inner need—to discover her humanity, femininity, and maternity—getting that baby is exactly what she wants. She doesn't know it yet—but she will.

We see this a lot, an opening door that looks great to a character's outer need, and terrible to his inner need, or vice versa. In *Father of the Bride*, Steve Martin's outer need is to keep his little girl from growing up. In this light, he dreads her impending wedding. But since his inner need is to accept her adulthood, her wedding is just the right crucible in which to forge a new relationship.

In *Everybody's Dream Come True*, Albert's outer need is to be a successful inventor, and his inner need is to acquire his manhood. The door opens when he meets barnstorming aviatrix KATHRYN HILLS, who wants him to build her a racing plane. He's getting his shot at inventing, but will he be up to the challenge? He's in the soup. Funny thing about the opening door: One way or another, it always seems to lead to the soup.

As you write down your opening door, remember to keep it simple: The door opens when he joins the circus; the door opens when she meets the boy next door; the door opens when they find a sacred amulet; that sort of thing. Again, if you can't boil it down to a sentence, you don't have a fix on the information yet.

THE HERO TAKES CONTROL

Having found this beautiful, beckoning door, the hero strides boldly through, ready for any adventure . . . or tentatively through, filled with trepidation. Whatever his thoughts going in, he immediately starts to take over in his new and challenging world. He enjoys early success here, and thinks that things are really, really going his way. He doesn't know it yet, but it's only a surface triumph, the appearance of success.

In *Tootsie*, Michael Dorsey enjoys early success in his new role. He has fans, money, approval, everything he could ask for. Is his victory real? No, because it's not Michael Dorsey but Dorothy Michaels who's earning all the kudos and encomia. He has the surface appearance; "Not triumph, an incredible simulation!"

In *Romancing the Stone*, the hero takes control when Joan Wilder arrives in Colombia and hires Jack Colton. She makes real progress toward her goal, and as things now stand, she has every expectation of success. Expectations, as we know, are made to be defeated. Otherwise, the story would go like this: A nervous young woman goes to Colombia to rescue her sister. She does. The end.

Not much of a story, is it?

In *Everybody's Dream Come True*, Albert takes control by building Kathryn's plane. When it flies, he thinks his story is over. If he were right, then she'd fly the plane, win a big air race, join him on the cover of *National Geographic*, and that would be that.

Why isn't this real success? Why is it only surface success? Because the thing that Albert *really* wants, his inner need of self-respect, has not been addressed yet. He hasn't been tested to the limit of his ability. In a very real sense, he hasn't yet earned his wings.

So when you're deciding how your hero takes control, think in terms of *early success* and *surface success*. Make things good for your good guy here. Make him enjoy what's happening. Give him a fun time. Above all else, make him unaware of the greater battle that looms ahead.

In *Star Wars*, Luke takes control by going off to join the rebel alliance. Along the way, he learns the rudiments of being a Jedi knight. Early successes make him think that he's learned it all. He knows there's such a thing as the Force, and he knows it's alive in his life, but he really doesn't know how to use it. In one sentence, we'd say that the hero takes control when Luke goes off to find the princess and gets introduced to the Force.

In *Big*, Tom Hanks takes control by moving to Manhattan, getting a job, an apartment, and all the other trappings of adulthood. He seems to have realized his dream of being "big," but he doesn't have a clue what true adulthood really means. Real responsibility as yet eludes him, so his story has not yet been told. In a sentence: The hero takes control when he moves to Manhattan and starts behaving like an adult.

Meanwhile, back on television, Mary wants Ted and Lou to be better friends. The door opens when they agree to try. The hero takes control by inviting them both to dinner, and they seem to be getting along. You know that the story's not over. Something's bound to go wrong. It has to. It's that or fifteen minutes of commercials.

An episode of *Murphy Brown* might find Murphy with the strong outer need of landing an interview with a tinhorn dictator from some banana republic somewhere. The door opens when Murphy gets the interview on the condition that she treat the dictator with respect she doesn't feel he deserves. The hero takes control when she curbs her atavistic urges and conducts the interview on the dictator's terms. But we know that Murphy's not being true to herself, so her story is not yet told.

In the Gospels, Jesus's strong outer need is to help the poor. The door opens when he starts his ministry, and the hero takes control by performing miracles, acquiring followers, helping the poor. He hasn't yet addressed his inner need, so his story's not done.

How does your hero take control? Think of one event that completes the following sentence: "The hero takes control by . . ." In *Everybody's Dream Come True*, the hero takes control by building a plane that flies. In your story, the hero takes control by . . .

Now challenge yourself. Think of five different, smaller ways in which the hero takes control. These are the details of your story. You don't need them yet, but you will. In *Tootsie*, the hero takes control by signing his contract, buying new clothes, doing well on camera, becoming friendly with Julie, and standing up to Ron.

In *Everybody's Dream Come True*, Albert takes control by designing a plane, helping Kathryn test it, taking credit for the invention, feeling good about himself, standing up to the town bully.

In your story, the hero takes control by . . .

Again, don't worry if you're wrong or right. The whole point of this exercise is just to give you a better feel for the sort of events that take place when the hero is taking control. All you really need is the umbrella description of these events. In *City Slickers*, the hero takes control by going out west to act like a cowboy. Is it as simple as that? Sure is, pardner.

A MONKEY WRENCH IS THROWN

I once taught screenwriting as a second language to students from Egypt, Spain, and Bulgaria, a veritable world conference on story structure. They all spoke at least some English, because English, thanks to CNN and MTV, is the language of the world these days. But American idiom gave them fits. This, in turn, gave me fits, so used was I to teaching in the cultural shorthand of my milk tongue. When I say to you, gentle reader, "a monkey wrench is thrown," you know what I mean. But a literal deconstruction of "monkey wrench" yields "a device for twisting simians." Illuminating? Helpful? I think not.

For monkey wrench, then, substitute "a new, bad thing," because that's what happens in the story when the monkey wrench is thrown. A screw-up happens, a new threat arises, a new character enters, or a complication develops. In a murder mystery, the hero will be in control, feeling like he's got the case all but solved, right up to the moment when his prime suspect turns up dead. In comic stories, especially on film, the new bad thing that happens is a change in the hero's state of mind.

In television sitcoms, the monkey wrench is usually thrown at the *act break*, the moment just before the commercial when the hero realizes that things aren't going according to plan. In the example we've been tracking, no sooner has Mary negotiated her truce between Ted and Lou than a new, bad thing happens, not only renewing their hostilities, but escalating them and somehow making Mary a part of the fight. Suddenly she's hostile too. She's experienced a change of state of mind. In television terms, this is also known as *the moment of maximum remove*. At this moment, it dawns on the hero just how distant she is from her goal.

Remember that up until this moment, our hero has had things pretty much his or her own way. You find the monkey wrench in your story, then, by asking and answering this question: When does something go wrong?

In a comic story, the monkey wrench is usually thrown when the hero falls in love. Why is this a bad thing? Because it creates a dynamic and irreconcilable conflict between the character's original, self-serving goal and his new goal of winning his loved one's heart. All during the "hero takes control" phase of *Tootsie*, things go great for Michael Dorsey. He's moving closer and closer to his goal of winning respect as an actor. Actress? Acting person. But the moment he falls in love with Julie, he's sunk. It's impossible for her to love him as long as he's a woman. The longer he maintains his pretense, the closer he gets to his original goal, but the further he gets from Julie's love.

In *Romancing the Stone*, Joan Wilder has no problems (apart from getting shot at regularly) until she falls in love with Jack Colton. Now her desire to see her sister set free is in sudden and dynamic conflict with her desire to go after the treasure with Jack and win his heart.

In *City Slickers*, everything's going fine for Billy Crystal. He's ridin' the range, ropin' them dogies, drinkin' that chuckwagon coffee without a care in the world. Then he falls in love with Norman, the calf, and he's stuck. Now he has responsibility. He can no longer ride that range and sing them cowboy songs without a care. Out of loyalty to that li'l dogie, he's got to bring the herd home safe.

The key word is "loyalty." A character always starts out with loyalty to himself and loyalty to his goal. What happens when the monkey wrench is thrown is that the hero experiences *displaced loyalty*. Michael Dorsey displaces his loyalty to Julie. Billy Crystal displaces his loyalty to Norman. Luke Skywalker displaces his loyalty to the rebel alliance. This new conflict between original loyalty and displaced loyalty takes and turns the story on its head. Up till now, our tale has been a simple one of a character wanting something and going after it. When the loyalty gets displaced, suddenly the story is about a character wanting two things that are mutually exclusive. Irresistible force versus immovable object. Trouble.

Romeo and Juliet have no real problems until they fall in love. Robin Hood and Maid Marian. Oedipus and Jocasta.

In *Midnight Cowboy*, Jon Voight displaces his loyalty from himself to Dustin Hoffman. In *Paper Moon*, Ryan O'Neal displaces his loyalty to his daughter, and once that happens, he'll never be at peace until he squares what he wants for himself with what he wants for her. In *The African Queen*, Bogart displaces loyalty to Katharine Hepburn. In *Casablanca*, Bogart displaces his loyalty to Ingrid Bergman. In *Key Largo*, Bogart displaces his loyalty to Lauren Bacall. In *The Maltese Falcon*, Bogart displaces his loyalty to Mary Astor. Displacin' kind of guy, old Bogie.

Once you've got everything going your hero's way, pull the rug out from under him. Drop love on his head. Make him want two things and make it so that he can't have both. In *Everybody's Dream Come True*, Albert falls in love with Kathryn. His loyalty thus displaced, he can't be content to take sole credit for their invention, nor can he win her heart until he gives her her due.

How does your hero's loyalty displace? What monkey wrench can you throw into your story to make things impossible for your hero? Who can you put in his path to create conflict between what he wanted in the first place and what he wants right now?

Your answer might look something like this: *Paula's monkey wrench is thrown when she falls in love with Chris, making it impossible for her to marry Bill.*

To make this twist work, you obviously need a character for your hero to become loyal to. Now may be a good time to go back, invent such a character, and create a throughline for that character to follow. You'll be looking for your old friend Mr. Comic Opposite, the person who can give your hero the *worst possible time*. That's who you want your hero to fall in love with. Nice person, you.

Okay, let's recap using two fresh examples. In *American Graffiti*, Richard Dreyfuss plays a high-school graduate who wants to go to college. The door opens when he gets a scholarship. The hero takes control when he drives around town, enjoying his last night of freedom. A monkey wrench is thrown when he falls in love with the girl in the white Corvette.

In *Strictly Ballroom*, the hero is a young dancer who wants to make his mark on the world of ballroom dancing. The door opens when he starts to dance his own steps. He takes control when he finds a new partner to dance with. A monkey wrench is thrown when he falls in love with her.

I hope that you're starting to see that this throughline can be an effective way of boiling down a story, yours or someone else's, to its essence. One thing it's good for is revealing flaws. If, for example, you don't yet have a decent monkey wrench, you'll see it now. For my money, it's far better to discover story problems here at the start than to write 120 pages of rambling screenplay or 400 pages of a comic novel, only to find out later (and too late) that the script is flawed on the level of the story.

As an aside, if you want to break off an affair, simply take your future former lover to the movies and start analyzing a film out loud. "That's what the hero wants," you say, "and now the door opens, and now he's taking control. Oh look, look! Here comes the monkey wrench! Boy, I saw that coming, didn't you?" You'll be alone before the popcorn grows cold.

The hurling of the monkey wrench is only the first in a series of bad things that happen to our hero. He's had a fairly smooth ride up till now, but things are going to get bumpy from here on in, because, as William Butler Yeats promised in "The Second Coming . . ."

THINGS FALL APART

Remember what I said a few chapters ago about taking perverse pleasure in making a hell for your hero? Well, now is when your hell-making skills really come into play. Once the monkey wrench has been thrown, you really want to litter your tale with bad news for the good guy.

In *Tootsie*, things fall apart when Michael's contract is renewed, when Julie thinks Dorothy is a lesbian, when Julie's dad proposes marriage, when Jonathan van Horn makes a drunken pass, when Michael discovers that his contract is ironclad, and when Sandy feels betrayed. Life is hell.

Just as "the hero takes control" encompasses a series of positive events, "things fall apart" encompasses a series of negative events. The challenge of the throughline is to boil all that bad news down to one simple statement. How about this: Things fall apart when Michael becomes trapped in the role of Dorothy Michaels.

In our *Mary Tyler Moore* story, things fall apart when Lou and Ted turn their anger on Mary, blaming her for the problems that exist between them. In *Star Wars*, things fall apart when Luke is forced to battle Darth Vader. In *City Slickers*, things fall apart when Jack Palance dies, when the other cowboys leave, and when a savage storm threatens the success of the cattle drive; in short, things fall apart when Billy Crystal finds himself leading the cattle drive. He's caught in a trap of his own making.

This is a key phrase: *caught in a trap of his own making*. More often than not, as tension builds between your hero's original loyalty and his displaced loyalty, he discovers that somehow or another it's his own damn fault. Of course, the Ghostbusters aren't responsible for all those ghosts running loose in Manhattan, but their cavalier attitude, and their carelessness in letting the captured ghosts escape, lead directly to a trap of their own making.

Let's walk a new movie all the way through and see how it tracks to this point. In *The Bad News Bears*, Walter Matthau, the hero, wants redemption for mistakes in his baseball past. The door opens when he agrees to coach a little-league team. The hero takes control when he recruits Tatum O'Neal and turns the team around. A monkey wrench is thrown when he displaces loyalty to the kids and realizes that their goal of winning has become important to him. Things fall apart when his own bad attitude (the trap of his own making) causes the players to lose faith in him.

Substitute Emilio Estevez for Walter Matthau, and hockey for baseball, and you have *The Mighty Ducks*.

Which raises an interesting point. Many successful comic stories have the same structure, so you might think that there's no original thought out there at all. In one sense, you're right. In terms of theme and structure, in terms of the way a story is told, we comic writers get led again and again to the same authentic places. This is not a bad thing. If you know anything about pop music, you know that most hit songs are written in major keys. If they're not written in major keys, they don't sound like hit songs. It's as simple as that. Likewise, if your story isn't structured conventionally, it doesn't work like a conventional story. Does this mean vote no on unconventional stories? Of course not. It's just that conventional stories, conventionally structured, are far, far easier to write, and to read, and to enjoy.

The trick, of course, is to transcend the structure with new and interesting comic characters, with inventive and amusing details, and with plot twists that make the conventional story uniquely your own. Just because *The Bad News Bears* explored the theme of redemption through baseball doesn't mean that there's no room for a movie that explores the theme of redemption through hockey, or a story like *Hoosiers*, which explores redemption through basketball.

Tell me if this wouldn't work: *Birdies!* (I'm making this up) is the story of a former world-class badminton player who molds some ragtag children into a badminton powerhouse. The hero, Twyla Hengst, wants redemption for mistakes in her badminton past. The door opens when Twyla has to teach badminton to the misfit kids. The hero takes control when she convinces them that "there's beauty in the birdie" and starts to shape their skills. A monkey wrench is thrown when she displaces loyalty to the kids and signs on to their dreams of victory. Things fall apart when Twyla is offered a shot at the Olympics, which would mean leaving her team in the lurch.

Will it be funny? Sure—if the characters are real comic characters in strong opposition, if exaggeration and clash of context are present, and if the characters' strong comic perspectives allow funny words and actions and situations to emerge. Does it matter that this ground is familiar and well-trod? I think not. As Pablo Picasso said, "You just keep painting the same picture over and over."

Which brings us back to our stories, yours and mine. In *Everybody's Dream Come True*, things fall apart when Kathryn accuses Albert of stealing credit for her inventions, when their plane crashes and Kathryn is injured, and when Albert faces the prospect of flying solo in an upcoming air race. In short, things fall apart when Albert realizes that he's going to have to see this plane thing through to the end.

Now do yours. First, list as many ways as you can in which things fall apart, and then boil them down to a single sentence.

You may find it useful right here to do what I just did with *Birdies!* Start over with a fresh, new idea and run it through the throughline. I think you'll find that it's easier to hit the marks the second time around. And the third, and the fourth. Eventually it will become almost automatic.

Here's another fresh stab:

The hero, a recent graduate from hotel-management school, wants nothing but a quiet little inn of his own. The door opens when he's hired by an international conglomerate to run a run-down resort in a Third World country ruled by a despotic strongman. The hero takes control when he goes to the Third World country and starts to turn the resort around. A monkey wrench is thrown when the hero falls in love with a beautiful guerrilla leader and displaces his loyalty to her. Things fall apart when the dictator comes to stay at the resort and the guerrillas plot to assassinate him by blowing up the hero's beloved hotel.

Can you see the conflict between our hero's original loyalty to the hotel and his new loyalty to the girl and her goals? As things now stand, something's got to give. When you move toward a moment when something's got to give, you're ready to start wrapping things up.

THE HERO HITS BOTTOM

There's an achingly beautiful moment toward the end of *Tootsie,* which takes place the day after Michael, as Dorothy, has made his pass at Julie, leading her to believe that Dorothy is gay. He comes to her dressing room to explain, but she won't listen. "I really love you," she says, "but I can't love you." In that instant, Michael knows that no matter what happens, as things now stand he'll never have the woman he loves, so he'll never really be happy again. Whenever I'm trying to remember how a hero hits bottom, this is the moment I grab.

This is the moment that a good story aims for. Having taken our hero out of his world and thrust him into a new and challenging one, having given him early success in that world, having displaced his loyalty, having made his situation bad, and then made his bad situation worse, we bring him at last to the moment of truth. Every story you've every loved, from *Sleeping Beauty* to *Moby Dick* to *Gone With the Wind*, has a moment of truth. For my money, the moment of truth is what makes the story real.

In our *Mary Tyler Moore* episode, the moment of truth comes when Lou hates Ted, Ted hates Lou, they both hate Mary, and Mary's not too keen on them. More to the point, it's the moment where Mary realizes that, unless something drastic happens, she's going to lose her two close friends forever. What's a girl to do?

In *Star Wars*, Luke is attacking the death star. Darth Vader is on his tail, and all his efforts to hit the target have failed. The voice of Obi Wan Kanobi comes to him and says, "Use the Force, Luke." To use the Force means surrendering his hard-won manhood to some higher power. Not to use the Force means to fail and die. What's a boy to do?

In *City Slickers*, the hero hits bottom when Billy Crystal's beloved calf, Norman, gets swept into the river. There stands our hero, with his conflicting loyalties laid out before him. On one hand, he can turn away from that calf and continue to live, which he desperately wants, now that he know what living really means. On the other hand, he can plunge into that raging torrent and try to save that calf, but he might die trying. As things now stand, he has no reasonable hope of a happy ending. What's a lonesome cowboy to do?

The common denominator to all these moments is the sense of time running out. The hero has come to the end of the line, the final moment when at last he'll have to choose between what he wanted when the story started and what he's come to want along the way. He arrives at a choice between his original self loyalty and his new displaced loyalty. It's a choice, in a sense, between "me" and "you."

In *Romancing the Stone*, Joan Wilder finds herself in a life-and-death struggle with Colonel Zola. At her moment of truth, as she battles for her life, she calls out to Jack Colton to come and save her. If he does, she knows that her dream of romance will be fulfilled. If he doesn't?

Then she'll die.

In *The Mighty Ducks*, Emilio Estevez hits bottom when his hockey team abandons him on the eve of the championship game. In *Birdies!*, Twyla hits bottom when her team abandons her on the eve of the championship game. In *The Bad News Bears*—well, you get the idea.

If your story is tracking right, you'll come naturally to the moment when your hero is poised between two things he really wants, two things which are clearly mutually exclusive. If Mary sides with Ted, she loses Lou. If she sides with Lou, she loses Ted. If Albert Collier gets in that crippled plane and flies, he might lose his life, but if he doesn't, then Kathryn never wins her race, and Albert never wins *her*.

By dragging your hero down to the bottom, you force him to make the ultimate choice. Use the Force or refuse the Force? Stay Big or be small? Be a woman or a man? Save the calf or save your life? These are the sorts of choices you want to make your hero face. And it's no accident that so many fine comic stories come down to a matter of life and death. As we'll discuss later, the greater the jeopardy, the greater the comedy, too.

So how does your hero hit bottom? Write that answer now.

If finding this moment seems difficult, well, yeah, it is. But it's vital that your bring your hero to a choice of this sort, or everything you've invested in the story up till now will be lost.

Surprisingly, it's less difficult if you take a fresh running start at the story. In my experience (and this is why I've bothered to go to such tedious length on the subject), the Comic Throughline often serves to reveal an otherwise obscure or uncertain moment of truth. Let's start with a new story and see if I can show you what I mean:

Frank, a thirteen-year-old boy in Milwaukee in 1968, has the outer need of being a hippie and the inner need of learning to sacrifice. The door opens when he meets a seventeen-year-old hippie chick who rocks his world. The hero takes control when he bonds with the girl, learns from her, and becomes, to outer appearances, a hippie. A monkey wrench is thrown when he falls in love with the girl and dares to believe that she might love him, too. Things fall apart when her draft-dodger boyfriend turns up and our hero gets dragged into their efforts to escape over the border into Canada.

Given this simple template, how must the hero hit bottom? Won't it inevitably come down to a choice between what the hero wants for himself—her love—and what he wants for her—her happiness? In concrete terms, he'll have to decide whether to help them get away, which means losing her, or to try and keep her for himself.

I must tell you that when I first wrote this throughline, I assigned the hero the inner need of learning true values. Looking at his moment of truth, I realized that the inner need of learning to sacrifice would make his ultimate choice that much harder to make. So I went back and changed his inner need to what you see above. That's how the system works. By laying out the story in its simplest terms, you can make changes on a rudimentary level, while such changes are still easy to make. Later, when you're writing the script or the novel or the teleplay, it will be much too late, and much too difficult, to change the story in a major way. Do it now while it's still easy.

Do it now with some fresh meat. Try a new story and see if it doesn't point itself inevitably toward some ultimate conflict. It won't all the time, and when it doesn't, you'll know that there are some key story elements still unknown to you. Or you'll know that the story you're chasing is a dog. The advantage is that you'll reach this understanding through the least possible effort, the smallest amount of actual writing. The Comic Throughline is the line of least resistance.

And what happens when the hero hits bottom? Facing his moment of truth, staring into his abyss, what does our hero do?

THE HERO RISKS ALL

With no certain hope of success, the hero in a comic story hurls himself into the abyss. He abandons his entire investment in his original goals, sacrifices everything for the sake of his displaced loyalty. The key here is that the hero does the right thing even if he doesn't know whether it will pay off.

With no certain hope of success, Billy Crystal throws himself into that raging river to save that drowning calf. He doesn't know if he'll succeed. He doesn't even know if he'll survive. All he knows is that things can't go on the way they are, and that, in this moment, he'd rather lose his life than fail to take the shot. Notice that it's just this sort of moment—one instant of genuine, authentic life experience—that he's been seeking all along.

With no certain hope of success, Michael Dorsey rips off his wig on national television and reveals Dorothy Michaels to be a man. In this instant, he doesn't know whether he'll win Julie's heart or not. All he knows is that he can't bear to live the lie another instant. He has to come clean.

So often in a comic story, the hero risks all by coming clean, telling the truth, confessing to the lie that's carried him through the story so far. Tom Hanks does it in *Big* when he admits that he's not an adult. Dorothy does it in *The Wizard of Oz* when she clicks her heels and says, "There's no place like home." She's admitting that she was wrong in wanting to leave home. Now all she wants is to have her home back. It takes a major leap of faith to risk everything on a pair of magic slippers, but that's what Dorothy does.

Luke Skywalker uses the Force. He doesn't know if the Force will work, he just knows that nothing else possibly can. He yields himself up to a higher power.

Mary Richards stands at her moment of truth, poised between Ted and Lou, loyal to both, and loyal to herself. Pushed to the end of the line, she finally shouts, "If you guys can't grow up and behave yourselves, I don't want to be friends with either one of you!" With no certain hope of success, she throws herself into the abyss. Is this a "strategy?" Does she hope that going ballistic will cause Ted and Lou to see the light? No. She just knows that she can't live this lie (approval of their feud) a single minute more.

She has to come clean. The fact is, she doesn't respect either of them any more, and she can no longer keep that secret.

Joan Wilder has her back to the wall, a knife at her throat. She calls to Jack, but Jack doesn't come. What will she do? If she waits for Jack, she'll die. When she can't wait a minute more, she abandons her lie—that she's a weak woman who needs a man to save her—and saves her own life. She throws off all her old notions of romance and comes into her own.

In *The Bad News Bears* and *The Mighty Ducks* and *Hoosiers* and *Birdies!*, the moments of truth are all the same. The hero says to his team, his loved ones, "I don't care about me, and I don't care about winning. All I really care about is you." In *Birdies!* as I see it now, Twyla will get all the way to the airport, badminton racquet in hand, ready to fly off to the Olympics. She'll see something that reminds her of her hopeful protégés and she'll realize, "I just can't do it." With no hope of winning back their loyalty, she'll bag her flight and rush back to the competition site.

In my story about the hippie wannabe, his moment of truth comes when he realizes that his loved one and her boyfriend will get caught unless he takes action. He risks his life to create a diversion. He has no certain hope of success, or even of survival. He has every reason to believe that his action will cause him to lose his loved one. But he knows that in the moment of truth there's nothing else he can do but sacrifice, thus fulfilling his strong inner need.

The moment of truth fulfills the inner need. In *Everybody's Dream Come True*, Albert's inner need is to acquire self-respect. In his moment of truth, when he overcomes his fear and flies that plane to victory, he's serving his inner need. In *Big*, Tom Hanks' moment of truth comes when he decides to go home. This fulfills his inner need of coming to terms with himself as a child.

Storytelling seems to be a mystery, but it can be like clockwork. If you know your hero's inner need, then you know what his moment of truth *must be*. If you know what his moment of truth is, then you know what his inner need *must be*. So ask yourself now, based on the story you've told so far, what must your hero do, what choice must he make or action must he take to fulfill the terms of his inner need? If all has gone according to plan, the answer will be obvious.

Again, to make this tool work best for you (and for the practice if nothing else), start over with a fresh idea and walk it all the way through.

The hero is an over-the-hill tennis star with the outer need to be a star again and the inner need to find the offcourt meaning of "love." The door opens when she must take on her comic opposite as her doubles partner. The hero takes control when she improves his game and they start winning. A monkey wrench is thrown when she finds she loves him, which is a problem because she already knows she hates him. Things fall apart when their tempestuous romance screws up their game and the partnership dissolves. The hero hits bottom when she realizes that she can win a tournament or win her man but not both. She risks all by giving up her shot for the sake of his love.

And what happens next?

WHAT DOES THE HERO GET?

They win the big doubles tournament. Our hero gets returned to glory and she also gets the man she loves. Oh, happy ending!

I argue with people all the time over happy endings. No, I do. People upbraid me in parking lots and say, "Hey, pal, why are you so dogmatic about happy endings? Why won't you admit that movies and TV shows and comic novels have happy endings just because that serves the marketplace? It's pandering!" Yes, they serve, but no it's not pandering. It's organic. The natural ending of a comic story is a happy ending. If it were otherwise, then all the comic currency earned by the tale would be forfeited by its outcome, sort of a substantial penalty for unpleasant withdrawal.

Moreover, the ultimate purpose of a story is to *instruct*, and the underlying message of any story is, "If you do a certain thing, here's what happens." If you kill your father and marry your mother, Oedipus, you don't get a happy ending. You have to pluck out your eyes and be miserable. But if you do the right thing and use the Force, Luke, you get rewarded. You destroy the death star and get to hang out with the princess for another two movies. Just one thing: She's your sister, so don't sleep with her or you might end up like ol' Oedipus there.

So yes, I'm a fan of happy endings. But I'm also a student of endings, both happy and sad, and I've noticed something very interesting about the endings in real comic stories. Not only is the hero a winner, he's a *double* winner, because what the hero gets is *both* his original goal and his new goal. Against all foreseeable odds, he manages in the end to serve both his self loyalty and also his displaced loyalty. Again, it doesn't have to happen this way, but because it does happen this way in so many stories, we ignore the compelling logic of such outcomes at our peril.

In *Star Wars*, Luke surrenders to the Force. Then what happens? He destroys the death star and acquires his manhood. He serves his ends and those of the rebel alliance. In *City Slickers*, Billy Crystal goes home with a renewed love of life and with the calf.

In a good comic story, the hero ends up with the best of both worlds. Joan Wilder gains both her self-esteem and the man of her dreams. Albert Collier gains both his place in the world and Kathryn's love. Mary Tyler Moore tells Ted and Lou to grow the heck up . . . whereupon they see the light, settle their feud, and meet Mary's twin needs of keeping peace among her friends and maintaining her self-respect.

Does this seem phony and forced? It certainly can be, if the sudden reversal of fortune isn't justified by what's happened before. But in a well-crafted story, the reversal is not only justified, it's the *only authentic outcome possible*. When Michael Dorsey reveals himself to be a man, he doesn't know that he's going to win Julie's love, but he *must* win Julie's love, because *revealing his true self* is the only action that could possibly achieve this outcome. He also gets work as an actor for the same reason: In risking everything for his own true love, he finally comes to understand himself. For the first time in his life, he is the sort of actor who can get work. Paradoxically, nothing could bring him to this pass but the ultimate sacrifice of his career.

After the hippie wannabe risks his life at that border crossing, the girl and her boyfriend escape safely into Canada. He's achieved his first goal: to understand the meaning of sacrifice. But has he achieved his second goal? Does he have the woman he loves? No . . . not until she comes back across the border, tells him Canada's too cold for her, and drives him off to Woodstock.

It turns out that his sacrifice, and only his sacrifice, could make her see his quality and win her love.

If this sounds like the gospel of happy endings, well it is. But I put it to you that if you set out to write an authentic comic story without an authentic happy ending, no one will be satisfied. Not you, not your readers or viewers, not even your mother, who's sworn the Oath of Writers' Mothers to love every word you ever put to page.

Try it. See if I'm wrong: Our hero is a struggling young writer whose outer need is fame and glory but whose inner need is to discover what being a writer is really all about. The door opens when he gets the chance to masquerade as a famous novelist at a writers' conference. The hero takes control when he pulls off the charade, passing himself off as the novelist. A monkey wrench is thrown when he falls in love with a woman who, in turn, passionately loves the person he's pretending to be. Things fall apart when a rival threatens to reveal his identity. The hero hits bottom when he's forced to choose between love and glory, between continuing the masquerade or finally coming clean. The hero risks everything by closeting himself in a room, writing a 200-page confession, and laying it at her feet. He has no certain hope that she'll forgive him or understand. He only knows that after all these lies, he has to tell the truth.

What happens next? What does he get? Is he thrown in jail? Banned from publishing forever? Sentenced to grim obscurity and misery? I don't think so.

No, check that, I don't *hope* so. Rather, I hope that the woman will forgive him and that his act of redemption, writing that confession, will teach him what it really means to be a writer and open the door to authentic fame and glory, the sort of reward that genuine good work brings. That's the ending that feels right. And because it feels right, I submit that it *is* right.

But, really, how long does it take to beat a dead horse? You'll find out for yourself what kind of endings your comic stories want to have. Just be aware that a happy ending is the icing on the comic cake, and if you don't give your audience the whole cake they may feel cheated. And don't be surprised when the happy ending creeps in.

Before we leave the Comic Throughline, I'd like you to run through it at least one more time. Choose any story you've worked with up till now, or choose a new one. If all has gone according to plan, you'll find it far easier going now than it was some umpteen pages ago.

So. Who is the hero? The hero is . . .

8
MORE TOOLS FROM THE TOOLBOX

Welcome back to all you joke crackers, column scribblers, cartoon scrawlers, and striders of the comic boards who dodged the last couple of chapters like the draft for an unpopular war. If story structure bores you stupid, you'll be pleased to know that the worst is over, at least until we get to the chapter on situation comedy, and you may feel free to ignore that one, too.

In this chapter, we'll look at some small, delicate tools that everyone can use. Where the last two chapters dealt with global strategies for comic storytelling, this one will focus on local tactics for improving your jokes as they appear on the page, or on the stage, or in smoky comedy clubs in the dead of last call.

THE RULE OF THREE

If you're like me, you spent most of ninth-grade geometry class in a desensitized torpor resembling nothing so much as a good, sound sleep. If you're not like me, then perhaps you're what we used to call a "vector dink," someone for whom the squaring of a hypotenuse or the bisecting of an angle held endless, pointless fascination.

I remember only about two things from freshman geometry. One is that Claire Franklin learned not to wear a bra that year, and the other is that two points define a line. Delighted though I was by the former, it's the latter that has served me well since the comic *ursprache* of my youth.

Two points define a line. A line presents a direction. Direction implies expectation: "If I continue in this direction, I'll move farther along this same line." Well, it turns out that we can craft a joke just by creating and then defeating that specific expectation. This is not news; you've seen this kind of joke a million times before. By another name, it's known as "setup, setup, payoff." Here are some examples.

> *I was teased about the typical stuff in high school: My height. The size of my nose. Oh, and that unfortunate arson conviction . . .*

> *All the great writers kept a journal: Gertrude Stein, Joyce Carol Oates . . . Dear Abby.*

> *"New MIRRO-GLO dissolves rust, polishes chrome, and gets your teeth an incredible white, white, white!"*

Each of these jokes is built on three iterations of an idea or theme. The first iteration presents the theme. The second iteration validates the theme like the second point defines the line. The third iteration violates the sequence. *Introduction, validation, violation.* The joke comes when the third item in the sequence cuts across the line established by the first two points and creates laughter in the explosive defeat of expectation.

It's almost like an IQ test question: Which doesn't belong in this set—a forklift, a backhoe loader, or a tea cozy? To make the rule of three work for you, simply find two things that belong to the same set, and then find something that extravagantly doesn't belong.

In *Bill and Ted's Excellent Adventure*, Bill and Ted tell us that Beethoven's favorite musical works include Handel's *Messiah*, Mozart's *Requiem*, and Bon Jovi's *Slippery When Wet*. The first is a piece of classical music. So is the second. They establish the line of "things classical." The third item could be any piece of music that's not classical, but the further removed it is (by exaggeration), the funnier the payoff will be.

Why two setups? Why not one? Why not three? Well, if you only have one setup, the audience doesn't have enough information to form a positive expectation which the payoff can then defeat. And if you have three setups, it's just redundant. If you said, "Handel's *Messiah*, Mozart's *Requiem*, Verdi's *Aida*, and Bon Jovi's *Slippery When Wet*, you'd be giving more information than people need. The third setup only drains tension from the moment, which correspondingly dampens the potential for comic release. So avoid redundancy. Don't over-explain. Try not to repeat yourself yourself. Let's run a few samples through the old setup-setup-payoff mill, shall we?

Setup	Setup	Payoff
deaf	dumb	ugly
jealous	greedy	Republican
coffee	tea	nerve gas
Deep Throat	*Deep Throat II*	*Bambi*

Now suppose we apply another tool, the inappropriate response, to the rule of three. In this case, we'd want the two points that define the line to have in common a certain "appropriateness of response." The third point will cut across the line with a wildly inappropriate response.

Three things you should never do at a football game: Cheer for the visiting team; curse in front of children; pour cold beer on big drunk guys.

Three things you should never say to the widow at a funeral: "He looks so peaceful." "He's gone to a better place." "He was great in bed."

Three things you should bring to an I.R.S. audit: copies of your tax returns, all your receipts, a small-caliber weapon.

Also remember that any time two voices or characters agree, then any third voice or character who disagrees in an exaggerated or inappropriate way creates a comic opportunity.

The rule of three is not my favorite tool. It often appears to me, as I'm sure it seems to you, that this rote repetition of setup, setup, payoff routinely comes out feeling forced and, well, unfunny. Personally I prefer found art, like that revelation about Claire Franklin's bra (damn well-found art at the time), but the rule of three is a handy little item to have in your back pocket. Forced and artificial as it may seem, it's often the shortest route to a joke.

Or if not a joke, a jokoid.

JOKOIDS

Jok•oid *n*. Not a joke, an incredible simulation.

A jokoid looks like a joke and sounds like a joke. It walks, talks, acts, feels, and smells exactly like a joke, except for just one little thing: It isn't funny. You would think that jokoids serve no purpose in your work. You would think that jokoids are to be avoided at all cost. You would be wrong. In writing comedy, in making a page of prose or a scene in a script funny, in working out a new routine on stage, or sketching out a new cartoon, there may be no tool more useful than the good old ugly ducking jokoid. And why might that be?

A jokoid fills the place on the page where a genuinely funny joke will eventually go. It's an interim step between no joke and the final, polished product. Maybe the jokoid isn't funny because the wording is wrong or the drawing is unclear. Maybe the exaggeration isn't extreme enough. Maybe the reader is asked to work too hard—or not hard enough—to get the joke. But when you go to repair a jokoid, you're merely doing corrective surgery under local anesthetic. That's far easier than crafting a perfect joke on the first try.

It's always easier to rewrite. It's always easier to create a finished cartoon from an imperfect preliminary sketch. It's always easier to polish existing material than to cut flawless new material from whole cloth. When I'm writing the first draft of anything,

I give myself total license to put any damned jokoid down on the page. Later, when I'm rewriting, I go back and examine those jokoids more closely. I ask myself what, in abstract, is the funny idea I'm going for, and then find new language to express the comic idea more strongly. That's how I turn a jokoid into a joke.

> *How many Amish does it take to screw in a lightbulb?*
>
> *Two—one to screw in the lightbulb and one to wonder what it's for.*

That's an okay line. Here's a better one.

> *How many Amish does it take to screw in a lightbulb?*
>
> *What's a lightbulb?*

In the first version, the reader *observes* the Amish person. In the second version, the reader *becomes* the Amish person. The element of remove in the first version takes the edge off the line. It's a jokoid. But it leads to the joke. That's its job. (As an aside, I've always thought the Amish were a great target for TV comedy. One thing's for sure—no letter-writing campaigns.)

Here's a joke:

> *A man's commitment to women's liberation wilts in the face of a wet T-shirt.*

Which grew from this jokoid:

> *A man's commitment to women's liberation lasts until the next bikini comes along.*

Why is the first line stronger than the second? Because the truth and pain of the joke ("men are scum") comes in a slicker package, with sharper detail and more visceral kick. Sometimes turning a jokoid into a joke is merely a matter of changing some nouns around.

If a joke isn't working, then, it may not need replacing but only adjusting. Trouble is, how are you going to know whether a joke works or not if you don't commit it to the page or the stage? This brings us all the way back to fear and the ferocious editor. By embracing the jokoid, and by recognizing that even unfunny things can become funny once they're open to inspection, we give a new and easy goal to our creative process. We want jokes, but if we'll settle for jokoids, we'll naturally feel more willing to take a shot. Jokoids give you the freedom to create unfunny comedy. A very useful freedom indeed. Why not exercise that freedom now? Write five lousy jokoids and see if you can rewrite them into true jokes.

We'll talk later about how to edit your work and how to develop and trust your own sense of what's funny and what's not. For now, just trust that the jokoid is your friend.

THE DOORBELL EFFECT

Have you noticed how in certain situation comedies, Dad or Mom or Chip or Sally will say, "We're okay now; everything's going to be fine *as long as that doorbell doesn't ring*" or words to that effect? Whereupon, with the relentless certainty of a loan shark circling his prey, the doorbell proceeds to ring. That's the doorbell effect.

I sure make it sound stupid, don't I? You'd sure be stupid to use it, wouldn't you? Not necessarily. With a little misdirection, a little tweaking of the jokoid, the doorbell effect can be a very funny bit indeed.

The character has a certain expectation—the doorbell won't ring—and then that expectation is defeated—the doorbell rings. The joke is funny as a function of the way it catches the character's expectation off-guard.

In *Monty Python's Life of Brian*, Brian is on the run from Roman guards and hiding out at the secret headquarters of the People's Front of Judea. Suddenly there's a knock at the door, and a dozen Roman guards burst in, search the joint, fail to find Brian, and leave. Brian comes out of hiding, and he's much relieved because he knows that, having just searched the joint, *there's no way in hell* those Romans will come back and search it again. Which, of course, they do. It's not the repetition of the gag, but the explosive defeat of Brian's—and the audience's—expectations that makes the moment so funny. Why the doorbell thing seems so lame in so many sitcoms is that the audience knows the joke so well that it no longer defeats their expectations.

To use the doorbell paradigm to comic effect, then, simply give your character a strong expectation of a certain outcome, make your audience believe that the expectation is valid, and then defeat the expectation as rudely and ruthlessly as possible.

Examples:

Expectation	**Defeat**
getting cash from an ATM	the machine takes your card—and your cash and wallet, too
driving home from work	you're stopped for speeding—by Glorxians
cool Christmas gifts	a stocking full of cheese
goodnight kiss	goodnight kick in the groin

Now you run a few.

If you're a stand-up comic, here's how to use the doorbell effect to create a sure-fire joke. All you do is stand on stage and "admit" (telling a lie to comic effect) that hecklers scare you co-matose (exaggeration). Then ask the audience please, please,

please not to heckle you. You create the doorbell expectation that they'll honor your request. Someone in that audience, in pure Pavlovian response, will obligingly provide the punchline by heckling you. It's a lock.

The doorbell effect is also a staple of the greeting-card industry.

> *I bet you're expecting some cash in this birthday card.*

> *I bet you're expecting the tooth fairy to deliver it, too.*

As an exercise now, try using the doorbell effect to create some jokes in your genre. Remember that it works best when it defeats the expectation both of your character and of your audience.

AVOID CLICHÉS LIKE THE PLAGUE

For jokemeisters like us, life is no bed of roses, no walk in the park, no day at the beach. It's a tough row to hoe, a bitter pill to swallow, a big hill to climb. But when the going gets tough, we put our noses to the grindstone and our shoulders to the wheel, because we know that time and tide wait for no man, and a rolling stone gathers no moss. We'd sell our own grandmothers to succeed because we know that nothing succeeds like success, and the early bird gets the worm, and a penny saved is a penny.

And the moral of the story? Avoid clichés like the plague. Any time you use a joke, or a common phrase, or a comic idea that's not uniquely yours, you run the risk of alienating your reader or your audience in a most unfortunate way. They'll bust you either for being so lazy as to borrow someone else's work, or so stupid as not to notice that you're trading in clichés. Either way, you lose.

It's easy to fall into clichéd patterns of writing. Things become so familiar to us that we imagine they're our own original thoughts. The best argument I can give against using clichés is this: A cliché is like a suit that you buy off the rack. Sure, it costs more money to buy tailor-made, but which looks better when you put it on?

As a habit of good writing, then, or good stand-up comedy or good cartooning or whatever, get used to policing your work to make sure that borrowed thoughts don't creep in. Sometimes it's hard to tell where original thought leaves off and poaching begins. If you're telling jokes about airplanes or sex or mothers-in-law, you're treading clichéd ground by definition. This just means that your jokes have to be that much more personal, that much more keenly observed. I know it's hard, but hey, I never promised you a rose garden.

But whatever doesn't kill you makes you stronger, and any landing you walk away from is a good one. By the same token, every cliché creates an expectation, in defeat of which you can create a joke, or at the very least a jokoid. If you start a phrase like, "You can't please everyone . . ." your audience or your reader has a rock-solid expectation of what comes next: ". . . so you might as well please yourself." If you finish that line with, ". . . so you might as well please your boss," or "you might as well please your wife," or "you might as well please me," you get the double benefit of having avoided a cliché and having defeated an expectation.

> Marry in haste, repent in Reno.
> The decision of the wife is final.
> On a clear day you can see the smog.
> Today is the worst day of the rest of your life.
> Don't bite the hand that feeds your ego.
> I never kiss on the first drink.
> A fool and his money are soon partying.
> Close only counts in horseshoes and simultaneous
>   orgasms.

And that's just the tip of the icebag! You can twist clichéd situations the same way you twist clichéd phrases. If you're writing a car chase, don't put it on a street. The darn things always happen on streets. Put it where it doesn't belong, like on a container ship, or at the zoo, or in a department store. You benefit from avoiding the cliché, from defeating the expectation, and from clashing the context.

Same thing with characters. The most clichéd character becomes funny if you imbue him or her with an attitude that's wildly inappropriate to the nature of his or her cliché. If your character is a beer-swillin', stogie-smokin' hard-hat redneck good ol' boy who'd just as soon spit on you as look at you, yet who nevertheless happens to raise prize peonies and read the works of Emily Dickenson (in authentic Victorian ball gowns) on open-mike night at the local bohemian hangout, you've taken a cliché and turned it on its head.

As an exercise, write down some cliché phrases and see what you can do to twist them around. Then take several cliché situations and try the same thing. I think you'll discover that the mere act of deconstructing the cliché will create some pretty darned exciting comic possibilities.

When all is said and done, after the dust settles, the bottom line is this: Clichés are both pitfalls to avoid and opportunities to embrace. When the Lord closes the door, he opens a little deli.

THE RUNNING GAG

A running gag doesn't run in place. If you're going to use the same joke again, you have to bend it, tweak it, or take it in a new direction in order to win your reader's heart or your audience's loyalty. Why should this be?

Jokes, as we know, are built on surprise, the unseen twist, the suddenly defeated expectation. Say a joke once and it's funny. Say it again and it's yesterday's news. So unless you change a joke when you repeat it, you offer your audience no new surprise by which to be delighted. As Queen Victoria so apocryphally put it, "We are not amused."

How do you twist a joke to make it new? There are several ways. One involves changing the *detail* of the joke. In *Murphy Brown*, the running secretary gag is always the same—Murphy can't find a secretary who works—but it's also always new. One week the secretary is an obsessive talker, the next week an illiterate or a Satan worshipper or a closet novelist or an escaped convict or the former president of a banana republic. The structure of the joke never changes, but the substance always does.

In *Star Wars*, there's a running gag about Han Solo's spaceship, *The Millennium Falcon*, and this quirk it has of not shifting into hyperdrive on command. The first time we see this joke, there's no real threat associated with its failure, but with every subsequent appearance, there's escalating danger. Here the running gag is changed by the altered circumstances that surround it. The *joke* is the same, but its *importance* has increased.

Another way to change a running gag is to assign the same line or attitude to a different character. The catch phrase in *Catch-22* is, "That's some catch, that Catch-22." Sooner or later, everyone in the book speaks this line, and it's a different joke every time, because whoever says it gives it a different meaning. To some it's a vexation, while to others it's a thing of beauty. Changing the source, then, can keep a running gag alive.

Sometimes the mere passage of time makes an old joke new. Woody Allen opens *Annie Hall* by telling a joke about a man who thinks he's a chicken. He ends the film with the same joke, but it carries a lot more weight now, because we've been through the hero's journey with him, and we understand the joke on a different, much deeper level.

What happens when time is not measured in hours but in weeks? Then you have television, a medium built on creating an expectation, and then meeting that expectation again and again, relentlessly, week after week after week, past cancellation and syndication, and on into the Running Gag Hall of Fame.

When people tune in *Saturday Night Live* each week, they expect to see someone like Dana Carvey's the Church Lady screwing up her face and saying, "Isn't that special?" Everyone knows it's coming. They can't wait to see it again. It turns out that a certain fixed percentage of a certain type of audience seeks not the new thing but the familiar thing. They want the same "buzz," the same triggering of their laugh reflexes that they enjoyed last week and the week before and the week before that.

So sometimes running gags *do* run in place. And the very best of them run all the way into the collective memory of pop culture. They cease being lines and turn into icons. Remember T-shirts with Jimmy "J.J." Walker saying, "Dyn-O-Mite!" or the Fonz saying, "A-y-y-y-y," or Bart Simpson saying, "Don't have a cow, man"? There's a certain lowest-common-denominator thinking about this kind of comedy. You almost never see T-shirts quoting T.S. Eliot, "I grow old, I grow old, I shall wear the bottoms of my trousers rolled." A shame.

Seek, then, the opportunity to hammer home your funny line, to create within your audience or your reader the expectation that the funny line will come around again. The best of all possible worlds, of course, is to set up that expectation and then defeat it by presenting your catch phrase in a new and different way, like one of those outlined above. In *Cheers*, it's a running gag that everyone shouts, "Norm!" when Norm Peterson enters the bar. Then someone gives him a setup line, and Norm cracks a joke. We know *something's* coming, but we never know what. Thus is the audience's expectation met and bested at the same time.

I have this pet theory that all human experience can be reduced, in one way or another, to creating and meeting repeatable expectations. We seek the same sensations, whether laughter or risk or exploration or sexual pleasure or gratification of the taste buds or what-have-you. For more on this subject, please see my essay, "The Unified Theory of Chasing the Buzz," published in monograph by the *Journal of Esoterica and Obliquity.*

Not.

CALLBACK

In using the word, "not," above, I continued a running gag established by Mike Meyers and Dana Carvey in *Wayne's World*. The astute reader will no doubt bust me for trading in clichés. If I may be forgiven, I did so to introduce another comic tool, the *callback*.

Close cousin to the running gag, callback works by direct reference to an earlier joke or idea. In *Tootsie*, Julie asks Dorothy why she uses so much makeup, and Dorothy alludes to a "mustache problem." Later, Julie kisses Dorothy and says, "I feel that mustache." That's callback.

Callback is a marvelously effective way to finish, or "button," a scene or a story or a comic essay or a screenplay or even a comic novel. At the end of *Silence of the Lambs*, Hannibal Lecter tells Clarisse that he's "having an old friend for dinner." In calling back to his cannibal habits, Lecter buttons the movie, giving the story a wonderfully fulfilling (not to say filling) sense of closure.

Suppose you're writing a comic essay about how much you hate to trim the hedge. You might recount how you grudgingly geared up for the job, but had no sooner started than you accidentally nicked a finger with the clippers. So you went inside to put on a Band-Aid, slipped on a wet floor, and sprained your ankle. You went to the hospital for x-rays, had an accident en route, wrecked your car, broke an arm, and put yourself out of commission for ten solid weeks. If you wrapped up the whole affair by saying, "At least I didn't have to trim the hedge," you'd be using the tool of callback.

In fact, why just *suppose* you're writing a comic essay? Why not do it for real? Fill in the blank: "I hate to _____" and write a brief prose piece that ends up by referring back to something in the first paragraph. If nothing else, this will give you clear awareness of where your essay will end, and that's an awareness of no small utility.

9
PRACTICAL JOKES

Of course, no book on comedy would be complete without a comprehensive discussion of practical jokes.

10
COMEDY AND JEOPARDY

There is a strong causal connection between comedy and jeopardy: The greater the jeopardy, the better the comedy. The more trouble your comic characters are in, and the more they have at stake, the greater your opportunity to create real and lasting comic moments. If you don't believe me, just think about the last time you rode a roller coaster. What did you do when the ride ended? Laughed, I'll bet. Or maybe barfed.

The reason for this is found in a concept I introduced earlier, *tension and release*. Just as a little tension can generate a little laugh, a whole pile of tension can create a big ol' pile of laughs. This is true whether we're speaking of Bart Simpson running from his dad in mortal terror, or Dorothy Michaels fending off the rape attempt of Jonathan Van Horn, or Yossarian facing death in World War II, or Holden Caulfield experiencing existential psychic meltdown in *Catcher in the Rye*. If you really want to make your audience laugh, make your hero sweat. A lot.

In *Lethal Weapon 3*, Danny Glover is stuck in a runaway truck with a lusty lady truck driver who has the hots for him. The joke is structured around her wildly inappropriate response, her exaggerated passion in comic opposition to his fear. But what makes it truly funny is that it takes place in the context of a life-and-death struggle. The audience feels incredible tension, wondering whether Danny will survive. That tension underlies and informs the scene, making the driver's every leering line much funnier. Danny Glover has a hell of a time, but for the rest of us it's a joyride.

The guys in *Ghostbusters* start out running a harmless little paranormal investigations service. By the end of the movie, a giant marshmallow man is ravaging Manhattan, and the safety of the entire city is at risk. This is called *raising the stakes*. Do it every chance you get.

If you have a character winning a trophy, attach a cash prize, too. If your character knows someone with a disfiguring disease, make it the character's best friend, or better yet, the character's mom. If your character cheats on his taxes, make sure he cheats big, gets caught, and stands to lose *everything* in the audit.

You see this in situation comedies all the time. Let me invent a new one now and show you what I mean. In the imaginary sitcom *People Like Us*, the comic opposites are a street-wise city kid and his bumpkin country in-law. In this episode, Country tries to cure a cold with a home-brew cold remedy that gets him "TV drunk." That's bad, but not as bad as it could be. Suppose City's up for a new job and he's bringing his prospective new boss home for dinner. Now Country's behavior has a huge and direct impact on City's fortune. This raises the stakes of the story.

There are two general ways to raise the stakes for your hero. One is to increase the price of failure, and the other is to increase the prize for success. In *Trading Places*, Dan Aykroyd's Winthorp falls from privilege. With nothing less than his whole way of life at stake, he has *a lot to lose*. Meanwhile, Eddie Murphy's Billy goes from outsider to insider, from con man to competent man. With nothing less than a great new life at stake, he has *a lot to win*. The stakes are raised in both directions at once, and every time they are, the story becomes richer in comedy. Let's see how this is done.

THE PRICE OF FAILURE

There's a guy playing roulette in a Las Vegas casino. He's got two bucks down on double zero, a grand in his wallet, a loving wife by his side, and a house back home that he owns free and clear. We don't care about the outcome of his puny two-dollar bet because there's no price for failure. Whatever happens, our boy can't lose more than two bucks here, and to him two bucks is nothing. There's no tension in the scene. No tension equals no release. No release equals no laugh.

Now suppose that the guy's betting not two dollars but two

thousand. Already he has *a thousand times as much to lose*. But wait, let's make the bad situation worse. Suppose it's the *last two grand he has in the world*. Suppose, further, that he's in debt to the marinara people to the tune of sixty grand, and the only way he can get even is if his 35 to 1 longshot pays off. To make matters worse (always, always make matters worse), there's a brute waiting for him outside, and the brute is called "Fingers" because that's what he likes to break first. *As if that weren't enough*, this poor guy has promised his daughter ballet lessons; no, knee surgery; no, a *lung transplant*, and how's he ever going to pay for that now?

Here's a guy with *everything* riding on that bet. There's so much tension in the scene that the audience is practically begging to laugh, just to ease the tension. This is what you want. Insofar as possible, put your comic characters in situations where if they lose, they lose it all.

This works for more than just comic storytelling. Remember the example I gave in chapter eight about the stand-up comic who pretends to fear hecklers? What if the comic makes it clear to his audience that his price of failure is really, really high? "If you heckle me, I'll have a nervous breakdown and spend my next five days in a closet, my next five years in therapy, and my next ten lifetimes trying to undo the psychic damage you do here tonight." He's raised the stakes. He's built tension. When the inevitable heckling comes, the explosive release of laughter will be that much greater.

In *Good Morning, Vietnam*, Adrian Cronauer's radio routines are funny in direct proportion to the escalating heat he takes from the Army, and to his escalating emotional investment in his Vietnamese friend and in the woman he loves. In *Cat Ballou*, Jane Fonda becomes responsible not just for herself but for her new-found friends. In this way the price of failure is increased.

Making a bad thing worse, then, means mentally shopping for more ways your comic character can be hurt by failure. Not surprisingly, this tool works well as a list.

Suppose your character is trying to get cash from an ATM. To raise the price for failure, you want to increase the *bad consequences* of his not being able to get that money.

He won't be able to buy the latest *People* magazine.
He can't take out his girlfriend.
He won't impress his boss.
He'll miss an (already long overdue) alimony payment.
Street people will harass him.
A gunman will kill him.
The world as we know it will come to an end.

You may not be able to see an immediate connection between cash and the end of the world. I could draw that connection (something about terrorists, plutonium, and a treasure map in a second-hand book store), but it's not necessary. Logic and comedy are not always close friends, nor often even nodding acquaintances.

Always remember that genuine raising of the stakes takes place on an emotional level. The closer you can get to a character's deep inner fears, the greater his or her real risk will be. In the example above, I listed a robber and an ex-wife as possible threats to our hero. Though the robber carries the greater physical threat, the ex-wife probably wields more emotional clout. Hint: To get the best of all possible worlds, make the ex-wife and the robber one and the same.

Try it. Setting logic aside, and going for her emotional core, consider a situation in which a young woman is trying on a dress in a boutique. What ten horrible things will happen if the dress doesn't fit?

Let's take another situation. You're writing a sketch about an actress with stage fright. Once you've put her on stage, how can you make her bad situation worse? What can you think of that would make yielding to stage fright hurt her worst of all?

First let's exaggerate her stage fright so that it's not just anxiety but full-on cataleptic fear. Next, place important people in the audience: agents, producers, friends and relatives. The more people she wants to impress, the worse her catastrophic collapse will be. Give her allies, people who have a vested interest in her outcome. If there are other actors, and maybe a writer or a director who are counting on her to deliver a *bravura* performance, she has that much more to lose by disappointing them. Still not satisfied? Throw in a stalker who's holding her daughter hostage backstage and will kill if he's not moved by her performance. *Now* we're talking risk!

Try it one more time. There's a photographer who wants to take a picture of a reclusive star. How can you raise the stakes to make his price of failure horrifyingly high?

It's not always obvious how the threat of dire consequence drives a comic scene. It may be that the threat is only *implied*. Gilligan, for example, faces the direct threat of not getting off the island, but also the implied threat of not pleasing the Skipper. Because this second threat is closer to his emotional core, it provides the sense of jeopardy that drives the comedy forward.

When we speak of jeopardy, though, we're not always speaking strictly of a bad thing. The more *hope*, as well as fear, that your character invests in an outcome, the more jeopardy he feels. Giving your character greater need for, or hope of, a positive outcome is called increasing the prize for success.

THE PRIZE FOR SUCCESS

In *Casey at the Bat*, the Mighty Casey strides to the plate with every expectation of hitting the home run that will inscribe his name forever in the pantheon of heroes. He has no fear of failure, but his need for success is almost unbearably high. Not just his hopes, but those of his teammates, the fans, followers of the Mudville Nine, indeed, the hopes of right-thinking people everywhere rest squarely on his broad shoulders. Ultimate triumph, for him and for everyone, is only a swing of the bat away.

In *Groundhog Day*, life becomes hell for Bill Murray not because he fears living the same day over and over again but because he hopes so much to win Andie MacDowell's love. And things become funny to us in direct proportion to how hellish they are for him. Remember what we said earlier about a moment not being funny to the person inside that moment? Often that person has so much hope and need invested in the moment that he just can't see the joke. It's a sad, pathetic place to be—which is exactly why it's where you want your characters to go.

Let's return to that scene at the ATM. We've discussed how to raise the price of failure. How could we also raise the prize for success? What *good consequences* could result from our hero extracting cash from that ATM?

> He'll buy a winning lottery ticket.
> He'll take his kid to a baseball game.
> He'll meet the mortgage on his house.
> He'll take himself to a museum, meet an artist, connect
>   with her on a deep emotional and spiritual level,
>   fall in love, get married, and live happily ever after.

And all because he got cash out of an ATM. Wow. Now go back and look at your photographer again. How can you raise the prize for success, so that success in snapping that photograph will redound to his huge and lifelong benefit?

It's hard to find the humor of a scene just by asking, "What's the humor of this scene?" But it's easy to ask, "What's at stake?" And when you know what's at stake, you'll know what's funny, too. People laugh because they care, because they *feel* your character's urgency and desire. If nothing's at stake in a scene, if it's just some yabbo at an ATM getting cash for dinner and drinks, the scene won't matter enough to be fun.

Hope for success and fear of failure go hand in hand in scene after scene. You may say, for example, that a character who *fears* to run into a mobster also *hopes* to *avoid* that fate. This is true. It happens that hope and fear are two sides of the same coin. The best situation of all is when overwhelming, unbearable, excruciating hope and mind-numbing, soul-killing, shorts-soiling fear exist side by side in the same character at the same moment.

In *Catch-22*, poor Yossarian clings to the hope that he'll finally fly enough missions to get sent home. At the same time, he fears that they'll raise the number of missions again, and he'll die before he achieves his goal. Hope and fear live side by side in our characters, just as they do in us. As they say, art irritates life.

STORY LOGIC VERSUS STORY DYNAMIC

As you try to make your characters' bad situations worse, you'll frequently face the nagging fear that you're not being logical. After all, every time you say, "As if that weren't enough," you're at least admitting the possibility that it *is* enough. Sooner or later, you start to strain credibility.

Or do you? Does your reader or your audience really want your story to be logical and rational? Remember that every comic premise presents a pre-existing gap between real reality and comic reality. In a sense, logic is written out of the equation, and credibility shredded, before the story even starts. If your premise is that a mermaid can move to Manhattan (*Splash*), your audience has already suspended its disbelief. They don't want logic, they just want laughs.

So when you're confronted with a choice between *story logic* and *story dynamic*, always make the boldest, noisiest, most dynamic choice, even if it beggars credibility. Exaggerate hope and fear, jeopardy and risk, just as you exaggerate comic attitudes and attributes. You may think you've gone too far, but I'll bet the price of this book you're wrong. Too much is never enough; you can always make a bad situation worse.

Readers or viewers can have two possible reactions to a given comic moment. They can say, "I don't buy that" or they can say, "I can't *believe* that." The former is laced with disdain, the latter with wonder. Obviously, you'd rather evoke wonder than disdain. Well, story logic doesn't serve wonder; outrageous storytelling does.

There's a classic moment in *Raiders of the Lost Ark*, when Indiana Jones is challenged by a Semite with a scimitar. The Arab's dazzling swordsmanship bodes doom for our hero, but Indy calmly takes out a gun and blows the guy away. There is no story logic in this moment—where did that gun come from anyhow?—but it's a bold and dynamic choice. It leaves the audience laughing and gasping and saying, yes, "I can't *believe* that." There's a similar scene in Ralph Bakshi's *Wizards*, in which wizards clash, one with black magic and the other with the comforting magic of a Colt .45.

We make logical choices because we assume that the audience wants them, but this is a false assumption. The best stories have so much boldness in their story choices and plot twists that the audience ignores or forgives lapses in logic. Comedy is not technical writing. If you build something genuinely funny, no one will care if there are a few pieces left over.

To sum up comedy and jeopardy, then, take the unfocused, unproductive question, "How can I make this scene funny?" and replace it with a simpler, smaller, detail-driven question, "How can I raise the stakes?" Next, divide that question in two: "How can I raise the price of failure?" and "How can I raise the prize for success?" Break those questions down into specifics: "What several outcomes might my hero fear?" "What several outcomes might he crave?" End by asking and dismissing the question, "Is it logical?"

Once again we've taken a mystery and rendered it comprehensible merely by asking and answering the right kinds of questions. Jeez, if you're not funny by now . . .

Perhaps you just need a few more tools.

11

STILL MORE TOOLS FROM
THE TOOLBOX

Most of what I know I learned from watching *Jeopardy*. The trouble is, I know almost all of it in the form of a question. "Who were Isis and Osiris?" "What was *Crime and Punishment*?" "Where is the Rugby Hall of Fame?" "When was 1789?" Last night, *Jeopardy* taught me the names of the five so-called "simple machines": the lever, the pulley, the inclined plane, the wheel-and-axle, and the screw. After these simple machines came more complex and intricate ones: chainsaws, dustbusters, clap-on clap-off light switches, etc. This is the way of things: Having nailed the basics, we humans inevitably start hotdogging. Still, while I'm not sure the world really needs a cordless screwdriver (since screwdrivers were cordless already), I do think that an advanced set of tools is useful to the practitioner of any craft. Of course, there's a fine, fine line between "advanced" and "obscure." Here, then, are the router and the awl, the Allen wrenches, as it were, of your Comic Toolbox.

MICROCONFLICT AND MACROCONFLICT

Often, the big conflict in your story is crystal clear. Indiana Jones has to escape the Temple of Doom, the prince and the pauper change places, Archie and Meathead hash it out. Often overlooked in our stories are the endless opportunities for small conflict. Putting these tiny skirmishes, this *microconflict*, into your work will move your comic storytelling to the next level of sophistication.

Suppose you have two brothers wrangling over the disposition of their father's estate. The big conflict, the *macroconflict*, is the battle of the will, and beyond that a battle of wills, in which the brothers' very destinies are at stake. Microconflict in this setting would be small tussles over who gets the Corvette, or who gets stuck with the ormolu clock, or whose pen they'll use to sign the will. Notice that the small conflicts reflect the big conflict. What's being played out thematically is also being played out in the moment.

A stand-up comic is telling the story of his jaywalking arrest. The large conflict is man versus law. Small conflicts might include the comedian mocking the policeman's haircut, or a run-in with a drunk in a holding cell, or getting fingerprint ink all over one's Armani suit. The big theme, man versus law, resonates through all the small conflicts.

A nun is running a brothel. Her big conflict is, "How do I save these fallen women?" Her small conflicts might include discomfort with casual nudity or foul language or dirty jokes. In a very real sense, when it comes to conflict, the pieces make the puzzle.

There's a poetic term for this: *synecdoche*, the part standing in for the whole. (*"What is synecdoche, Alex?" "That's correct, please select again." "Okay, Alex, I'll take 'Rhymes with Orange' for a thousand."*) A poet swept up in transports of synecdoche might refer to a flock of birds as "wings upon the air." Now you might think that such a poet should be lined up against a mime and shot, and I might even agree with you, but still, to get the most out of your comic stories, you must milk your moments, letting small, on-the-spot conflict be the microcosm which reflects the macrocosm.

You can shoot the poet later.

Try this exercise: A woman is hitting on a man in a bar. Their macroconflict is her desire to score versus his desire to read the *New York Times*. List some microconflicts that underscore the major conflict in this scene. Think peanuts. Think pick-up lines.

In *Everybody's Dream Come True*, Albert's big conflict is his battle of wills with Kathryn. Their microconflicts include arguments over who's a better pilot, disputes over wing design, pitched battles over table manners, mocking one another's taste in poets, doubting each other's courage, arm wrestling and more. In your major current work, the macroconflict is _____

_____ and

the microconflicts are _____ .

If your character is having a bad day in a big way, don't neglect a single opportunity to give him a bad day in small ways, too. When a man loses his job, his wife, his best friend, his car, his home, and his prized collection of 1940s soda-fountain glasses, all on the same day, it only makes sense to have him step in dog poo, too.

EAR TICKLES

Ear tickles are words or phrases that sound pleasing to the ear or look good on the page. Ear tickles include alliteration ("What are words that start with the same letter, Alex?") internal rhymes, and puns.

Alliteration. Why does "Semite with a scimitar" sound better than "guy with a sword?" I don't know. Why do bright colors delight the eye? Some say that there's a survival reason for colors attracting the eye—they draw our attention to edible fruit or something. While I can't imagine that the ability to alliterate was passed down to us from our forebears by Darwinian selection, nevertheless it's true that alliteration does *something* we like, and letting your punchlines alliterate may make them, oh, say, 5% or 10% funnier.

All other things being equal, a line that alliterates is better than one that doesn't. But be aware that too much alliteration soon palls. What's worse, it calls attention to itself so that your cleverly turned phrase may actually detract from the emotional impact of your joke. By all means, add this skill to your toolbox, but use it judiciously.

Okay, right now (and this is your comic coach talking), drop and give me twenty—alliterations that is. If nothing else, it's a workout for your spelling muscles.

Internal rhymes. Consider the difference between the phrases "comic toolbox" and "levity toolbox." The first is a vowel rhyme. The "ah" in "comic" finds a complementing "ah" in "toolbox." In "levity toolbox," there's no such vowel, or internal, rhyme. Just like an alliterated phrase sounds marginally better to the ear, a phrase driven by an internal rhyme gets slightly better play. The distinction is truly minimal, but the careful and diligent comic writer seizes every opportunity to improve his or her words, no matter how marginally.

Notice that I could have used the phrase "humor toolbox" instead and rhymed the "ooh" in "humor" with the "ooh" in "toolbox." Which is better? No way to say. It's entirely subjective. One wonders, in passing, if internal rhymes are a survival skill. One thinks not.

As an exercise, go back to something you've written recently and see if you can add the filigree of internal rhyme to your work.

Puns. I'm not a pun-loving guy. I don't think they're jokes, or even jokoids; mostly, they just take up space where a real joke could otherwise go. Many writers and stand-up comics and cartoonists confuse puns with jokes, and I think they do themselves a disservice. The best reaction you can hope for with a pun is a groan; the very best reaction you can hope for is a big groan. To put it another way, if puns are outlawed, only outlaws will have puns.

A pun is a word or phrase bent or twisted in such a way that it suggests something new without leaving its original meaning completely behind. A pun gives a reader or listener a little puzzle to solve. Twist the phrase insufficiently and the puzzle solves itself. Bend the phrase too far and it becomes impossible to solve.

Whether a pun works or not depends largely on whether the audience brings with it enough information to solve the puzzle. If you don't know the old National Rifle Association slogan, "If guns are outlawed, only outlaws will have guns," then you probably didn't get the pun above. That's okay with me. I don't want you to get too enthusiastic about puns anyhow.

Well, why not? Because a pun has no emotional content. There's no truth and no pain in a bent phrase. It's a verbal gymnastic and nothing more. It may demonstrate your cleverness, but it can't touch anyone's core. It's like being able to tie a knot in a maraschino cherry stem with your tongue. It may get you free drinks in bars, but it won't help you find true love.

All these elements—alliteration, internal rhymes, puns, plus "funny words," hard consonants, joke names, and other linguistic jumping jacks—must be handled with care. Though tweaking a phrase or substituting a "funny word" for a non-funny one can make a marginal joke marginally better, in no way can any of these small tools make a bad joke good or make an un-funny line funny. At best, they're sequins; at worst, they're tacky and self-conscious gaud.

I use these tools very late in the writing process, and then only if I'm sure that going for the ear tickle will in no way harm the real meaning of my line or my scene or my story. This whole class of humor calls so much attention to itself that it can end up ruining otherwise funny material. Still, it may be worth an extra 5%, and 5% is better than nothing.

DETAILS

Often the difference between a good comic moment and a great one is the application of detail to the picture. Why refer simply to a "dog" when you can identify the dog as a dyspeptic rottweiler with the words "Born to sniff crotch" branded on his haunch? Why have a character "walk" across a room when you can have him prance, or dance, or ooze like melting snow?

Detail helps your cause in two ways: First, it makes your story, sketch, routine, or essay much more vivid to the reader or listener. This draws people more deeply into your work, creating more emotional investment, and thus more tension, which you can release as humor. Second, actively going for detail gives you a keener sense and a clearer picture of your own work. Plus, detail is a self-improving tool. The more you seek to make your details really rock and roll, the better your details will become. Going for detail strengthens both the work and the worker.

Here's a paragraph built on ordinary nouns, verbs, and adjectives:

> A man drives down a street. At a stoplight, he pauses to light a cigarette, so that, when the light turns green, he barely misses getting hit by another driver running the opposite light. The man looks at his cigarette and says, "It's a lucky thing I stopped to light a cigarette."

Now watch what happens when we substitute for detail:

> A greaseball with a joke haircut tears down Spiro Agnew Boulevard in his teal green 1969 Dodge Daytona and careens to a last-second stop at the world's longest stoplight. He whips out a pack of John Player menthols, jams a butt between his pallid lips, scrapes a strike-anywhere match on the fly of his faded Levi's, and wraps himself in a fog of blue smoke and sulfur. The coughing jag lasts like a lifetime—almost as long as the light, which, after a glacial epoch or two, finally turns green. Because he's still hacking like a madman, the greaseball is slow off the line. He jets out—and then stands on his brakes a split-second before being creamed by some psycho in a Suzuki Samurai who clearly can't tell the difference between red lights and green. "Damn," says the greaseball, admiring his 'rette. "Who says these things are hazardous to your health?" He coughs up some phlegm and furiously drives on.

A couple of tools I used here were exaggeration and the will to risk. I'm much less interested in making the thing logical than I am in making it fun. And always, always, I'm asking myself have I pushed the material as far as I can? Should the cigarettes be regular John Players or menthols? Should the cars be a Daytona and a Samurai or a Hyundai and a LUV truck? This sort of work can be pleasant and relaxing. Since all I'm doing is simple substitution, one detail for another, the work can only improve. It's all gain and no risk . . . a creative person's paradise, as far as I can tell.

Which detail is "the best?" There's no way to tell. In the end, you just play God and use the details that delight you. The good news is that just as there are no absolute right answers, there are no wrong ones either.

Here's another plain-brown paragraph. Please rewrite it for detail. The interesting thing is that no two people will come up with rewrites that are even remotely alike.

> It's the start of daylight-saving time. A woman wakes up in the morning and goes around her house resetting all

her clocks. She resets the clock in the kitchen and the clock in the living room and the clock in her bedroom. The telephone rings. It's her mother, asking her if she remembered to reset her clocks.

Like some of our other tools, detail is subject to overuse.

You can get so caught up in detail that you lose sight of your story or your drawing or the point you were trying to make. Particularly in screenplays and teleplays, there's a fine, fine line between amusing detail and distracting detail. Heap on too much arch detail in your scene direction, for example, and you'll only take the reader off the page, calling attention to your cleverness instead of your story. It's not easy to capture just the right amount of detail, but it's always easier to go too far and then pull back than it is to push ordinary stuff to new limits. So give yourself license to go too far. Detail, not variety, is the spice of life.

THE EYEBROW EFFECT

Red Skelton used to do this routine where, in the process of putting on clown makeup, he applied eyebrow pencil to his eyebrows. He accidentally made the right eyebrow just slightly larger than the left, so he'd correct the problem by adding some pencil to the left eyebrow. This, inevitably, made that eyebrow just slightly bigger than the right. So he'd add some more to the right, then the left, then the right, and so on until his eyebrows extended up over his forehead, down the back of his neck, and on into the next county. For reasons which are no doubt clear to you, astute reader, we call this type of joke "the eyebrow effect."

How can you use the eyebrow effect in your own work? Simply by setting up a situation where the solution to a problem creates a slightly larger problem, the solution to that problem creates a larger problem, which creates a larger problem still, and so forth and so on, straight over the horizon.

Suppose you have a bumbling comic murderer trying to remove his fingerprints from a crime scene. He starts by wiping all polished surfaces with a handkerchief. Then he realizes that the handkerchief has his monogram, so he decides to burn the handkerchief. He sets it alight, but the fire gets out of hand and spreads to the curtains, setting off a smoke detector, which emits a piercing scream, which wakes the neighbors, who call the fire department. Now he's got a raging fire on his hands, and the authorities are on the way. Trapped by the blaze, he uses a fire extinguisher to create an escape route for himself. Outside the building, he hurls the fire extinguisher back into the blaze, only to realize that now the fire extinguisher has his fingerprints on it. In a desperate effort to eradicate physical evidence from the scene, he plunges back into the blaze, where he dies a fiery death, proving once again that crime—especially stupid crime—does not pay. This tool is a specific application of "making a bad thing worse," one in which the comic character makes his own bad thing worse, and then worse, and then worse and worse again. Two other things to notice are the relationship of comedy to jeopardy in this small moment and the fact that the sequence is comic to us but deadly serious to the person trying to clean up his own mess.

All you really need to trigger this sequence is a comic character whose flaws will allow him to stumble into an eyebrow situation. That is, he has to be stupid enough, or scared enough, or stubborn enough, or desperate enough to get into this particular type of trouble. A bumbling murderer works; so does a flaky short-order cook, or an incompetent house painter, or a perfectionist chemist. Just add detail and you're golden.

Try this one: Imagine that your hero is a janitor at a nuclear power plant. He's accidentally locked his lunch in the broom closet. See if you can "eyebrow" him from that broom closet to a full-core meltdown.

It's possible for the eyebrow effect to motor a whole comic story. Consider a time-travel tale in which the hero hits his thumb with a hammer, goes back in time to un-strike the blow, creates a small change in history, tries to correct it, creates a bigger change, tries to correct that, and so on until the very survival of mankind hangs in the balance. A little eyebrow goes a long, long way.

VIRTUAL HUMOR

The best lines in comic writing do three truly marvelous things: They tell the story, tell the truth, and tell a joke, all at the same time. I call this kind of line a *three-dimensional (3-D) joke*. They're not easy to write, but they're worth their weight in twenty-pound bond.

There are two ways to approach 3-D jokes. One is just to write intuitively and hope for "found art" along the way. This works better than you might imagine, because by the time you're deep into your story, with a full and complete understanding of your comic characters, they tend to start doing and saying things that are authentic both to their nature and humor and to their story. If they're well-built comic characters, they'll naturally be funny as a function of their comic perspective. If your story is soundly constructed, then the events of that story will naturally move it forward. If you've paid attention to the theme of your work, then the truth will naturally emerge.

The other way to approach the 3-D joke is to attack it a dimension at a time. If you've written a line that does nothing but move the story forward, go back and rewrite it so that it tells the story *and* tells a joke. Then rewrite it again so that it tells a truth as well. Because this breaks your creative problem down into separate, smaller problems, it makes your creative task that much easier. Of course, this requires a strong commitment to rewriting and also a strategy for understanding the inner workings of your story, your scene, and your line. We'll discuss the commitment to rewriting later. As for the strategy, one I find useful is *virtual humor*.

When I'm trying to create 3-D jokes in a scene, I strip it down to its essentials. What I want is to see the humor, the story, and the truth, all on an abstract level.

Suppose I'm writing a scene in which a diva is trying to seduce her hunky stage manager. By virtual humor, I abstract out the story of the scene: A woman is using power for seduction. I abstract out the truth of the scene: Women can be as exploitative as men in the right circumstances. And I abstract out the humor: Her efforts will fail because he's just too dim to understand what she's trying to do. With this abstract understanding, I can look at any moment in the scene and see how to make the moment function in three dimensions. She takes off her blouse, say, and whispers, "I suppose you know what this means." "Sure," he answers. "Costume change."

In my description of the guy at the stoplight, the abstract story was that of a man stopping to light a cigarette. The truth was that he's a jerk and shouldn't be smoking. The joke was that the deadly activity actually saved his life. With this abstraction of the scene, a behavior coupled to an attitude and an irony, we could rebuild the scene a dozen different ways. Try it and see.

The trouble with our scenes, a lot of the time, is that we don't actually know what's going on in them. Virtual humor can reveal much that was hidden. If you're stuck on a scene or a joke or a cartoon, or just trying to get more out of it, abstract it down to its essence, and then rebuild it to comic effect.

Suppose I want to make a joke about how I hate cats. Instead of just floundering around looking for a funny line, I ask myself first what's the "story" of hating cats. I want cats to stay away. What's the truth? Cats can be annoying. What's the joke? My hatred of cats manifested inappropriately. Looking for the 3-D joke, then, becomes a matter just of searching for the intersection of these sets. I want cats to stay away, and I find them so annoying that I'll pursue that goal in a wildly inappropriate way: thus, "The only good cat is a doorstop."

Go back and re-examine some comic piece you've created lately. Select a paragraph or a scene or a sketch or a drawing and write down in plain English the point you're trying to make, the story you're trying to tell, and the joke you're trying to crack. At worst, this will reveal what elements are missing. At best, it may lead you to a more elegant solution to your comic problem.

Is it really possible to find good jokes this way? You may have to be the judge of that. All I know is that when I'm frustrated by a scene that I *know* could be funnier, or deeper, or more useful to my story, I start by asking what's this scene, story, or joke really about? I find this a far more useful question than, "Why won't the damn thing work?" or "Where has my sense of humor gone?" or "What's the best way to slit my wrists?"

BUILDING AUDIENCE ALLEGIANCE

Whether it's one reader curled up on her couch with your comic novel, a dozen people thumbing through your cartoon book in a bookstore, 2,000 people watching your stage show, 10 million avid viewers tuned in to your hit sitcom, or a whole wide world watching your movie, your audience is your friend. Earn their allegiance and they'll forgive a multitude of sins. Violate their trust and they'll turn on you like a dyspeptic rottweiler with the words "Born to sniff crotch" branded on his haunch. There are a couple of ways to win their loyalty and a couple of ways to lose it. Let's examine them in turn.

One thing an audience looks for is *consistency.* They want to know that the rules of your comic world are going to stay the same, and not jump around in an arbitrary and artificial way. Comedy requires understanding. They have to get your joke in order to "get" your joke. If you confuse them with inconsistency, they will feel betrayed. And they will leave.

For example, if you've written a story that takes place in a foreign country, where people know nothing about American culture, you can't suddenly throw in a joke about McDonald's. If those foreigners know about McDonald's at all, they must know about McDonald's all along.

If your comedy is farce comedy, it has to be farce comedy throughout. You can't set it in motion as a realistic romantic comedy and then start throwing pies in people's faces. Your audience's gears will grind. Maybe you'll re-establish contact, but maybe you won't. If you don't lose them, you won't have to face trying to win them back.

And the thing is that an audience, from a single reader to the entire global village, is incredibly sensitive to shifts of this sort.

Because the human mind craves order, an audience wastes no time in establishing its own gestalt of your world. They understand intuitively what the rules are and feel subconsciously violated when those rules are broken.

It's also vitally important to give your audience sufficient information. As we've discussed, telling a joke is presenting a little puzzle to be solved. If your readers or viewers don't have all the clues they need to solve the puzzle, they'll feel stupid and inadequate, and they'll take it out on you.

Here's an example:

> *I'm Jewish, but I grew up in California. You know what the technical name for a California Jew is, don't you? Presbyterian.*

What's the virtual humor of this line? West Coast Jews are a lot less religious than other Jews elsewhere. By exaggeration, they're so much less Jewish that they're actually Christian. Using detail, we substitute Presbyterian for Christian, because Presbyterian is a more sharply focused word. But none of this works if you, my audience, don't know that California Jews are held to be less religious than other Jews. If you don't have enough information, the joke is lost.

Of course, it's possible to supply your audience with enough information to solve the puzzle. In the example above, I could pitch the joke this way: "I'm not saying that California Jews aren't religious, but their technical name is Presbyterian." The puzzle contains its own clues for solution.

Notice also that I'm careful to identify myself as Jewish before I make the joke. I don't want people thinking I might be anti-Semitic. By telling you that I'm Jewish, I retain for myself the right to make fun of my own kind, and you continue to think of me as an okay guy.

This is called *avoiding an adversarial relationship.* In addition to knowing what your audience understands, you have to know what your audience will tolerate. In these politically correct times, for example, certain types of racist or sexist humor are (thankfully) déclassé. It may be that in the next ten years it will become the banner of bad taste to refer, say, to internal-combustion engines or the former Yugoslavia. The savvy comic writer stays abreast of these changes. You don't need to pander to your audience, but you don't want to alienate them, either.

Unless, of course, alienation is your act. Plenty of stand-up comics have built their success entirely on having an adversarial relationship with their audience. How can this work?

All comedy *creates an expectation* within an audience. A "shock" comic like Howard Stern creates the expectation of bad behavior. When he then meets that expectation, he's not alienating his audience, but rather giving them exactly what they want. By meeting their expectation, he wins them over completely. An insult comic is expected to be rude. By creating and then meeting the expectation of alienating his audience, he actually earns their approval.

It turns out that meeting an audience's expectation is about the single most useful thing a comic creator can do to win an audience's allegiance. Violating that expectation, on the other hand, is the kiss o' death. As we discussed above, changing the rules leaves an audience feeling confused and betrayed. Violating their expectations is a big way of changing the rules, and it's very upsetting to an audience. Especially a TV audience.

When people tune in an episode of, say, *Married . . . with Children*, they have a certain hope and a certain expectation. Their hope is that Al Bundy will win, but their expectation is that he will lose. While the show can defeat their hope, it must not defeat their expectation.

Why can you defeat a hope, but not an expectation? Because "hope" is our picture of how things should be, but "expectation" is our picture of how things really are. By violating an audience's expectation, you're telling them that they're wrong, somehow. People don't like to be wrong.

Which doesn't mean they don't like to be surprised. If you can meet your audience's expectation and defeat it at the same time, you've really got them where you want them. In *Married . . . with Children*, the best of all possible worlds is for Al to lose . . . but lose in a completely unforeseen way. You want your insult comedian to piss you off in a new and different way. Howard Stern must reinvent shock every day if he wants to keep his fans coming back for more.

Of course, there are some people who hate Howard Stern, don't find him funny, and wish he'd get hit by a truck. Not everybody likes his material, and not everybody's going to like yours, no matter how carefully you shape and tailor it. If you try to be all things to all people, you'll end up being nothing to nobody. The bottom line is this: *Know your audience.*

There's a great scene in *This is Spinal Tap* where the band is mistakenly booked to perform at an Air Force dance. As a heavy-metal band, they can't please that audience no matter how hard they try. They simply don't have the right tools for the job. By knowing your audience, by understanding what they know, what they'll tolerate, and what they find funny, you'll be able to figure out how to amuse them, or even if you can amuse them at all. If you can't, don't sweat it. They're just stupid, and you can tell them I said so.

12

SITUATION COMEDY

Some people think situation comedies are easy to write. Some people watch really, really bad sitcoms on TV and say, "Hey, I could do better than that." And you know what? They're probably right. They probably could write sitcoms better than the bad ones. Trouble is, the television industry is already pretty well glutted with writers who can write bad sitcoms. The trick, if you want to succeed in that neck of the weeds, is to write sitcoms better than the *best*, not the *worst* of them. If this is your path, I hope this chapter will help you blaze the trail.

THE SPEC SCRIPT

The typical passport to the land of sitcom hopes and dreams is the speculative, or *spec*, script. This is a sample episode of an existing television show that you write to demonstrate your ability to capture the characters' voices, the story structure, and the jokes and rhythms of a given show. In choosing which show to write a spec for, there are a couple of things to keep in mind.

You want to choose a "smart" show. There's no point in writing a spec episode of a silly, bad, or derivative situation comedy, because no one who might hire you is the least bit interested in reading specs for that sort of show. You want to choose from among the hip, hot, "sexy" shows that are popular at the time of your writing. Here in 1994, the shows most often targeted for spec are *Frasier, Home Improvement,* and *Seinfeld.* But you need to know that by the time you read this book, all these shows will have been "specked to death" by the preexisting universe of sitcom wannabes. What you want is to get out ahead of the curve, pick and spec a show before it becomes a hit, and subsequently gets ground up in the spec sitcom mill. Watch the new sitcoms. Try to be the first on your block to write a spec script for a smart new show. At the worst, you'll write a spec for a show that doesn't become successful, in which case all you've lost is the time it took you to do the work, but what you've gained is the experience of having done that very work. About an even trade, I'd say.

As you choose your spec target, ask yourself if you like the show you're specking for. Will you sufficiently enjoy watching and studying it and writing it to devote the weeks and months of work necessary to do a good job on your spec script? Don't kid yourself here: There's no point in writing a spec script for a show you just don't like, no matter how popular or smart it may be, for the simple reason that you won't write the script very well. You may have a very serviceable, workmanlike approach to the writing of that spec, but some essential enthusiasm will be missing, and its absence always shows.

Play to your strengths. Do you have a knack for gags? Then you want to spec a gag-driven show. Do you have "heart?" Then you want to write a sample for a show that has lots of heartfelt moments. Can you write kids well? Write a kids' show spec. The purpose of a spec script is to knock 'em dead with your proficiency on the page. Do everything you can to give yourself an edge in that direction. It might be useful at this point to note your strengths (and weaknesses) as a writer. Not only will this help you choose the right show to spec, it will also show you in general terms where your craft needs work.

Finally, can you find your soul in the show? This is really the one key question. In my experience, no sitcom script is any darn good if the writer doesn't put his or her real heart, real feelings, and real emotion into the work. Does the show you've picked offer you this opportunity? If you feel no connection to the characters or the situation of the show, how can you invest your true self in the work? Like a lack of enthusiasm, an absence of heartfelt commitment will torpedo even the best spec effort.

LEARNING THE RULES

To make your spec script shine, you have to learn the rules of the show you're writing for, and then follow those rules in your own spec script. In the last chapter, for example, I mentioned a rule for *Married . . . with Children*, that Al Bundy always loses. To write a spec episode of this show well, you'd have to know, and follow, that rule.

On *Murphy Brown*, there's often a gag, or even a running gag, about a secretary, but the stories are never built around a secretary. Failure to follow a rule like this will betray your ignorance of the show's inner workings. It's a rule of *Mad About You* that the stories always turn on conflict between Paul and Jamie. In Bob Newhart's shows, there's almost always been a telephone monologue to showcase Bob's trademark strength with this gag. It was a rule of *Gilligan's Island* that no one ever escaped from the island. Can you imagine writing a spec episode of *Gilligan's Island* where they all got away?

For more on the rules of a show, contemplate what type of comic story the show tells. Remembering that *Taxi* is a center-and-eccentrics configuration would lead you to choose a story that placed Judd Hirsch at the center of an eccentric conflict. Then again, remembering that *Taxi* is off the air would lead you to choose a different show to spec in the first place.

You learn the rules of a show by reading sample scripts of that show and watching taped episodes. Read these scripts and watch these episodes over and over again, until you have an understanding not only of the show's form and structure but also of its hidden logic, its taste in stories, and its sense of humor.

A show's rules extend to all aspects of that show. Which character gets the main story? Who gets the secondary stories? Is someone a straight man? Do characters tell jokes and make wisecracks, or do all the laughs come from the characters' comic perspectives? What sort of language do these people use? What topics are taboo? Do they make reference to the outside world or do they live within a hermetically sealed sitcom bubble? Will given characters act the fool? To write a spec script correctly, you need all this information and more. It's not simply a matter of ready, aim, fire the pie.

SITCOM STORY STRUCTURE

Situation comedies are structured either as two-act or three-act tales. *Mad About You*, *M*A*S*H*, and *Married . . . with Children* are two-act structures; *Murphy Brown* and *The Simpsons* play in three acts. Each act ends with an *act break*, a big dramatic moment that (one hopes) creates a sense of expectation and dread strong enough to hold the viewers' interest across the commercial break and bring them back for more.

In a two-act structure, look for your act break to be a moment of maximum dread. At the act break, things should be as bad for your characters as they can possibly get. If your story is about a husband and wife fighting, then at the act break the husband is banished to the couch or the garage or the best friend's house. If your story is about characters trapped in the basement, then the act break is when they break a big pipe and the water starts to rise. If your story is about a character getting blasted on cough medicine with his new boss coming over, then the act break is when the boss arrives just as the cough medicine kicks in.

Not many years ago, some genius had the bright idea to divide the show into three parts and thus make room for extra commercials. By this logic, we'll soon have four-act and five-act sitcoms, and eventually twelve-act sitcoms, with commercials every two minutes. Be that as it may, in three-act structure, as in two-act structure, it's necessary for the moment before each commercial to have some real drama and urgency to carry the viewer over the break.

I like to think of my three-act act breaks in terms of *trouble is coming* and *trouble is here*. At the end of the first act, the characters know that a bad thing is looming. At the second act break, the consequences of that bad thing have been brought home. This second break corresponds roughly with the moment of maximum dread in traditional two-act structure.

In an episode of *Murphy Brown*, trouble might be coming in the form of a summons for Murphy to appear in court and reveal a confidential source. Trouble arrives when she's thrown in jail for not revealing the source. In an episode of *The Simpsons*, trouble is coming when Bart learns that he has to write a term paper by tomorrow morning, and trouble is here when he wakes at dawn, having fallen asleep in the middle of his work.

In any event, your act break or breaks must create a sense of expectation, a large, pervading, "Oh no!" feeling in your reader or your viewer. Here's where your skill at making bad things worse will really come in handy. Again we face the surprising notion that comedy is less about laughs than about willful, perverse destruction of a character's serenity and peace. Cherish this perversity and use it in your writing; if you use it in real life, they tend to throw you in jail.

No matter what happens in your story, remember that situation comedies are essentially circular; things always end up more or less back where they started. If a character gets fed up with his family and moves out of the house, clearly the act break is the moment when he leaves. Just as clearly, the story will end with the character having moved back home. Why this is so has to do with the episodic nature of commercial television. In the main, audiences return to a sitcom each week to see their favorite characters doing pretty much the same things they did last week and the week before that.

Which is not to say that there's no change in a sitcom story. In fact, there's a subtle and interesting change in every sitcom story, and understanding this change is the key to understanding sitcom story structure.

THE ARC OF STABILITY

Sitcom stories start out at a point of *old stability*, travel through increasing *instability*, and ultimately arrive at a *new stability*. You might have an episode, for example, where the old stability is that dad doesn't allow his daughter to date. Through increasing instability, dad and daughter have conflict over this subject. Dad forbids, daughter defies, dad discovers, daughter lies, etc. Finally you'd reach a new stability, in which dad and daughter agree that dating is okay within responsible and agreed-upon limits. (If this sounds like conventional sitcom morality, it is, but then again, a sitcom is just a mirror on the world; it tends to tell people exactly what they want to hear. If not, it tends to get canceled.)

To take another example, the old stability might be a

character's denial that she's growing old. Instability might come in the form of an accident or an illness or the death of a relative or friend. The new stability would be the character's realization that she is indeed growing old, but that's okay. The arc of travel from old stability to new stability is frequently a trip from *denial* to *acceptance.*

Notice how this type of story flows naturally from a point of departure to a point of maximum remove and back again to a point very near the original point of departure. Also notice that looking at your story on this level is a form of abstraction. Once you've identified an interesting old stability, instability, and new stability, you'll find literally dozens of stories to explore built in this same vein. Do yourself a favor and explore all these alternatives at length. Don't assume that the first solution is the best solution; always make room for the new idea.

Spend some minutes now and see if you can build some stories on a track from old stability through instability to new stability. I'll start you off.

OLD STABILITY: A husband and wife love each other.
INSTABILITY: They feel mutually unloved, underappreciated, and taken for granted.
NEW STABILITY: They rekindle their romance and love each other anew.

OLD STABILITY: A teenage boy is living at home.
INSTABILITY: He feels crowded by his parents' rules and moves into a bachelor flat with his buddies, where he discovers that independence ain't all it's cracked up to be.
NEW STABILITY: He returns home with a new appreciation for his family.

OLD STABILITY: A girl is in denial about her parents' death.
INSTABILITY: A pet dies, and at its funeral, the girl falls apart and finally opens herself up to grief.
NEW STABILITY: The girl achieves acceptance of her parents' death.

OLD STABILITY: A man has a job.
INSTABILITY: The man gets laid off.
NEW STABILITY: The man gets a new job.

This last example may seem absurdly elementary, but it's telling just the same. If you can't reduce your story to something *this simple*, then you don't fully understand it yet. Like the Comic Throughline, this sort of shortcut serves both as a point of departure for deeper story exploration and as a means of checking to see that your story has an authentic arc of change. Give it a shot.

OLD STABILITY:

INSTABILITY:

NEW STABILITY:

OLD STABILITY:

INSTABILITY:

NEW STABILITY:

OLD STABILITY:

INSTABILITY:

NEW STABILITY:

In the end, structure without substance is like a chocolate egg with no nougat center. To make your characters' changes of state interesting to the audience, you have to tell a worthwhile story—or two—and link them to a compelling, or at least an engaging theme.

A-STORY, B-STORY, AND THEME

Many, though not all, situation comedies slice themselves up into *a-story* and *b-story*. The a-story is the main story, the big problem, the heavy emotional issue with which a given half-hour of television reality chooses to concern itself. Typically, the a-story is given to the star of the show, the main character. Also, the a-story explores the theme of the episode. Whether that theme is, "tell the truth," or "be true to your school," or "don't do stupid things," it's played out in the largest, deepest, and most dramatic sense in the a-story.

The b-story is much smaller and lighter than the a-story. Usually involving secondary characters, it carries far less emotional weight and gets less screen time than the a-story. In a well-crafted sitcom, there's a thematic connection between the a-story and the b-story, in which the b-story comments on and amplifies the meaning of the a-story.

I like to think of the a-story as the melody and the b-story as the harmony. If your a-story had a certain Mr. Wacky hassling his boss for a raise, for example, then your b-story might involve Wacky's kids dunning him for a bigger allowance. If your a-story involved Wacky trying to kick his heroin habit, the b-story might involve his girlfriend battling a coffee jones.

Do the a-story and the b-story have to be connected in this way? No, of course not: In the a-story, Wacky goes to jail, and in the b-story, his cousin has a zit. Or it may be that the a-story and the b-story only intersect when one solves the problem of the other. For instance, if Mr. Wacky has a dilemma over whether to fudge his taxes, he might find the answer in forcing his daughter to do her own algebra homework rather than cheat off a friend. Are stories stronger if they're thematically linked? I think so. It's harder to get this kind of story right, but the reward is worth the effort.

ANOTHER SITCOM STORY SHORTCUT

Because not all strategies work for all writers, I'd like to introduce another quick-and-dirty way to get a line on your sitcom story. To use this shortcut, think in the following terms: *introduction, complication, consequence, and relevance.*

The introduction to a sitcom story is the thing that gets the trouble started or puts the tale in motion. An out-of-town guest arrives. An old girlfriend turns up. A first date looms. A driver's license expires. A vacation starts.

The complication is the thing that makes the bad situation worse. If the introduction is one character taking cough medicine, the complication is another character bringing the boss home for dinner. If the introduction is one character running for school office, the complication is another character entering the race. If the introduction is a character weaving a lie into an English essay, the complication is that essay winning a major prize. If the introduction is Mr. Wacky going to the doctor, the complication is discovering he only has three weeks to live.

The consequence is the result of the conflict created by the introduction and the complication. If two people are running for the same office, then the consequence is the outcome of the election. In the cough-medicine story, the consequence is when the cough medicine blows up, so to speak, in the boss's face. The consequence of Mr. Wacky facing death is his coming to terms with his mortality, only to discover (since we'd like to run the series for another five years or so) that he's not actually dying after all.

The relevance is simply a statement of the story's theme. And, by the way, a theme is best expressed as an imperative, and instruction, a call to action. Stand by your friends. Do the right thing. Don't fear the future. Stop and smell the roses. Accept your own mortality. Shower the people you love with love; that sort of thing.

Here's how an episode of *Gilligan's Island* might lay out. Introduction: An alien spacecraft lands on the island. Complication: Gilligan befriends the aliens, who agree to take him home. Consequence: Gilligan worries that the aliens will be exploited and lets them leave without him. Relevance: Do the right thing, even if it costs you.

Or suppose you had a sitcom called *Bed and Breakfast* about a couple's conflict over how to run their little inn. Knowing nothing about these characters and their lives, you could nevertheless construct a neat little four-sentence story for them.

Introduction: Buddy books his old frat-rat pals and their poker game into the bed and breakfast. Complication: Beth books a group of genteel bird-watchers for the same weekend. Consequence: Things get out of hand, and Beth and Buddy have to cooperate to manage the crowd. Relevance: Communicate!

You may think that storytelling of this sort is facile—all surface, no substance. Certainly you don't know everything you need to know about a story in four sentences. But everything you need to know is implied in those four sentences—if they're the right ones.

As an exercise, take an existing situation comedy, or make up one of your own, and see if you can crack some shortcut stories for that show.

My show is called *Mr. Wacky*, and it's about a former kids'-show host now running a retirement home for over-the-hill actors.

> Wacky sets up an illegal casino to raise money to pay off the I.R.S. The police bust the casino, and Wacky is thrown in jail. Wacky's impassioned courtroom defense beats both the gambling charges and the I.R.S. audit. Theme: Fight city hall.

> Wacky's doctor tells him to go on a diet. Wacky tries but fails to diet, and ultimately has a heart attack. During his near-death experience, he sees the error of his ways. Theme: Make your life count.

> Wacky goes on a game show, where he's a big winner. Then he discovers that the game is fixed. Sacrificing his new-found fame and fortune, Wacky blows the whistle on the crooked game. Theme: To thine own self be true.

This tool of shorthand storymaking (which works for all kinds of stories, and not just sitcoms) is especially useful when you're shopping for story ideas. If you generate a long list of stories developed only to the level of introduction, complication, consequence, and relevance, you'll know pretty quickly which are the good ones without having to do a whole lot of extra work.

Another thing to look for with this shortcut is what I call the *implied fireworks scene*. A well-structured sitcom story often suggests or implies a big, climactic scene in which all the fireworks explode or all the pies get thrown or all the hidden secrets get revealed. Just as you should be able to draw a line from old stability to new stability, in a well-structured story you can draw a clear line from your story's introduction to its implied fireworks scene.

If your story's introduction is a character taking home-brewed cough medicine, the implied fireworks scene is when the character acts outrageously in front of the worst possible person at the worst possible time. If your story starts with a lie, any lie, the implied fireworks scene is the one where the truth is finally told. Again, you can't know the details of the implied fireworks scene just in a sentence, but giving it a name tells you where to look for answers.

Often the implied fireworks scene turns on a *decision*, which turns out to be the key to the entire story. Suppose you had a sitcom about a retired pro football player. In a given episode, he might get a shot at returning to the game. Without knowing anything else about that episode, you can pretty well be sure that the implied fireworks scene will be the one where the footballer *decides*, once and for all, what to do about his lingering pro dreams. Old stability: Character feels that his career is over. Instability: Character gets one last chance. New stability: Character accepts that the past is, indeed, past.

Spend some time now working with these storytelling tools and find out which ones work best for you.

STORY OUTLINES

Before you write a sitcom script, you'll want to write a full and complete *story outline*. This document is a present-tense telling of your tale, incorporating as much detail, as much real emotion, and as much funny incident as you can cram onto the page. Typically, this piece of prose runs ten pages, more or less, but there's no hard-and-fast rule on length. You simply want to tell the story as completely as possible, for your story outline will be the blueprint from which you write the script.

Warning: If you're new to writing situation comedies, this is the part of the process you're most likely to overlook. Maybe you'll say, "Outline? We don' need no stinkin' outline," and you'll plunge directly into your script, confident of working out the story as you plug along in the script. Folks, take it from someone who's been there, that way lies madness. If you shortchange your time in outline, it will only come back to haunt you in script. Why? Story problems. By writing and rewriting and rewriting your outline many times, you'll reveal your story problems and then solve them as they appear. It is several orders of magnitude easier to fix problems in outline than it is to fix them in script for the simple reason that you have fewer words, and far fewer pages, to change. Do yourself a favor: Obsess on the outline; make sure the story works before you go to script.

Here's what a typical paragraph from a story outline might look like:

ACT ONE/SCENE ONE - WACKY LIVING ROOM - DAY

MR. WACKY is channel-surfing, marveling that all fifty-seven stations have managed to synchronize their commercial breaks. His teenage son, DWIGHT, comes in from school, acting nonchalant but obviously hiding something. Wacky pressures Dwight until Dwight reveals that a girl has asked him out on a date. This is bad? wonders Wacky. Is there something about Dwight's gender identification that Wacky ought to know? No, no, Dwight's a breeder; it's just that this girl has a "fast" reputation, and Dwight heard that she's only interested in his body. Dwight feels exploited. Wacky solemnly agrees that no one deserves to be treated as a sex object, but after Dwight leaves the room, Wacky pumps his fist in triumph: "Yes! My son's a stud!"

Once you've completed a first draft of your story outline, you want to examine it at length for two things: problems and opportunities. Problems are flaws in the logic or the sense of your story. Opportunities are all the myriad ways you can make the story stronger and more interesting, and its scenes funnier, livelier, and deeper, before you even get to script.

When dealing with story problems, you need to think in terms of two kinds of logic: plot logic and story logic. Plot logic is outer logic, the sequence of events that you, the writer, impose on your story. Story logic is the inner logic of your characters, the reasons they have for behaving the way they do. All of your story moves must satisfy both plot logic and story logic. In other words, your characters must do what they do to move the story forward, but their actions have to make sense to the characters themselves. If they don't, you end up with plot robots, characters who serve no purpose but to move the story forward.

Suppose you're writing a spec episode of *Mr. Wacky* (Are you? I'm flattered . . .), and you want Mr. Wacky to consider a vasectomy. He can't just wake up one morning and say, "Gee, I think I'd like to have my scrotum opened." Rather, something in the story has to drive him to this point. If his girlfriend has a pregnancy scare, Wacky may decide that the time has come to say goodbye to Old Mr. Spermcount. This sequence satisfies both plot logic and story logic; you, the writer, want to get Wacky into that hospital room, and now Wacky wants to get there, too.

If plot logic and story logic don't agree, your readers or viewers will feel dissatisfied. So as you rewrite your story outline, make sure that every move every character makes is justified by who that character is, what he wants, and how we understand him to behave.

Opportunities in your story outline are places where you can put your comic tools to work. In the example above, I put cynical Mr. Wacky in front of a television and let him react in his cynical way to *all those commercials* on TV. In rewriting the outline, I may see in this scene an opportunity to exaggerate Wacky's reaction or apply clash of context to Wacky's comic perspective, or even use abstraction to find a far better TV enemy. Home shopping? Televangelists? How can I make his bad situation worse?

It's in rewriting your outline that your story really gets good, and funny. Here's why: Every time you rewrite your outline, you go further into your story, you understand it better, and you can mine its comic potential more effectively.

I might be three or four drafts into my story, for example, before I realize there's even more fun to be had from Dwight having *two* girls after him, or from Wacky falling for the girl's mom, or from Wacky and his son going on a double date. The mere act of rewriting the outline inevitably makes the story richer and the characters more consistent, authentic, and interesting.

To make the most of your story outline, you have to write the darn thing, and write it again, and again, and again, until the problems all go away and the opportunities all emerge. Spend some time now—not minutes, but hours or days or weeks—writing and rewriting the outline for your next sitcom script. The more time you spend in outline, the better your eventual script will be.

STORY TO SCRIPT

If you've done your job in outlining your story, it should be fairly easy to write the subsequent script. Well, maybe "easy" is too strong a word. Maybe "not impossible" is the phrase we need. But consider this: Writing a script from a thorough and detailed outline is merely the act of translating a story from one form to another. Writing a script without a full outline is like panning for gold with a shrimp fork.

Does a well-wrought outline guarantee no story problems in script? I wish. Unfortunately, in going from story to script we often experience what I call *the Grand Canyon effect.* No matter how good the canyon looks from the rim, you really won't get to know it until you go down that donkey trail. No matter how thoroughly you've worked out your story, you won't discover all its problems until you hurl yourself into the script.

Your sitcom script should be more or less as long as those of the show for which you're writing. I once asked a story editor how long my script should be, and he said, "As long as you like, so long as it's not less than forty pages and not more than forty-two." These days I prefer a more organic approach. Write your story as fully and completely as you can. Cut out everything that's irrelevant to the story. More often than not, you'll end up with a script that runs about right.

If all else fails, mirror the scripts of the show you're writing for. Just do it like they do it, in format and length, and you can't go too far wrong. Professional presentation is important. Your spec script is your calling card; you want it to be your showcase. This means that your characters' names are spelled correctly, that your page layout is consistent and clean, that your copies are crisp, and that typos are eradicated. At minimum, you don't want to give anyone an easy excuse to say no. They'll find plenty of reasons to do that on their own.

You see, there's this phenomenon in Hollywood (and elsewhere, one imagines) called "the black hole of spec scripts." When you send your earnestly wrought spec script to an agent or a producer or a television show, it joins dozens, maybe hundreds of other, equally earnestly wrought spec scripts. It helps to form a pile of scripts that could conceivably be used for the construction of Doric columns. Eventually, someone will pick your script up off this burgeoning Babylonian tower. If the first thing they see is a typo, or the star's name misspelled, or photocopies of paperclips, they'll throw your script back on the stack and pick up someone else's script instead. It's cruel, but a fact: Your script can lie inert, in place, until the show gets canceled, or the producer passes on, or the agent gets sick of the business and retires to Palm Springs. You want to give your script every advantage in the competition to get read. Start by making it look good. Making it read well is a far harder proposition.

In these later days, when everyone and his dentist has written a spec sitcom, you might not even get a full read. Maybe they'll open it to a page at random and judge the whole work by what they read there. Think back to what I said about microcosm and macrocosm. Can you see that in order for your script to work as a whole, it must work *on every page*? Sometimes, unfortunately, one page is all you get.

Learn to test your own script rigorously and make sure that every page sings, and shows your real strength as a writer. Does that mean you'll get work in television situation comedy? Maybe. Maybe not. Those odds, unfortunately, are long, and they don't look to be getting shorter any time soon. Still, someone has to write the darned shows, the bad ones and the good ones alike, and if you have the talent and the drive, you may be the one. Just don't fool yourself into thinking that situation comedy is only about jokes. As you can see, it's about much more.

13
SKETCH COMEDY

Sometimes you don't want to tell a whole comic story. Sometimes you just want to open and explore a comic moment. If that's the case, you don't need the big comic structure of novels or screenplays, but you do need structure of some sort, if only to answer that nasty vexing question, "Where do I go next?"

You must know by now that I won't let you wander into this part of the comic planet without a map, or at least a set of coded instructions. This isn't the only way to write sketch comedy, but it's a nine-point method I find useful. Maybe you will too.

1. Find a Strong Comic Character

We're back to basics: Who is your story about? Use what you know about comic perspective, exaggeration, flaws, and humanity to create a comic character for the center of your sketch. Don't imagine that sketches are about "normal" people any more than any other type of comedy is. Think for a moment about your favorite sketch comedy and you'll see that it's built on *characters*: Lily Tomlin's Edith Ann, John Belushi's Samurai warrior, etc.

It's not enough just to invent a comic character and hold him or her up for inspection. This creates the static picture of a character who's all dressed up with nowhere to go. You have to put your character in motion. Comedy is conflict. Sketch comedy is comedy. Therefore . . .

2. Find a Force of Opposition

You have a couple of choices here. You can either find your character's comic opposite or find a normal character to be your comic character's foil. If your comic character is Ralph Kramden, he'll need Ed Norton to give him the worst possible time. But if your comic characters are the Coneheads, then merely introducing them to normal earthlings will provide sufficient force of comic opposition.

In any case, you want to make sure that all your characters have a strong desire either to *win* or to *get away*. Absent one of these motivations, they have nothing to fight about, and they'll just sit around making pleasant conversation. Your sketch will stop before it starts. Best-case scenario, you have two or more characters who want first to win and then to get away. What you need next is something to keep them from parting company until the battle is joined and fought.

3. Force a Union

What you're after here is *set glue*, a strong, compelling reason why your characters have to stay together on the set for the life of the scene. This forced union can be as benign as a fictional television talk show or as malign as a prison cell or a room in hell. Monty Python used to force the union just by having some unsuspecting person walk into a shop run by a lunatic. Bob and Ray made endless use of a radio interview format. Virtually any situation will do, so long as it's easier to get into than out of.

4. Escalate their Conflict

Sketch conflict starts small. Someone wants to know what time it is, and someone else won't tell him. Someone wants to buy furniture, and someone else won't sell it. Someone wants to take the coast route to Santa Barbara, and someone else wants to go through the mountains. No matter how the conflict starts, make sure that the argument gets worse (by which, of course, we mean better) almost right away. Make it loud and angry. Make it personal. Make it physically violent if at all possible.

The easiest way to escalate conflict is to push it toward your characters' emotional core. If a married couple is arguing over how to get to a party, it starts with "We're lost," then quickly escalates through "You never ask for directions" and "Stop nagging me" and "Why are you so stupid?" all the way to "I never should have married you in the first place" and "I want a divorce" and someone getting out of the car—preferably at highway speeds.

5. Raise the Stakes

At this point in the sketch, introduce a new element of risk or reward for your sketch characters. Make the scene be suddenly about something new, different, and fundamentally more important.

If your sketch starts out with a priest trying to save the soul of a fallen woman, the stakes get raised when she turns the war around and puts his celibacy at risk. If the sketch starts out with someone trying to sell a shoe shine, the stakes get raised when it turns into class warfare. Always ask yourself, "What's the worst possible thing that could happen to this person next?" and then find a way to make that worst thing happen.

6. Push the Limits

Make the bad things worse. If you have a fallen woman propositioning a priest, introduce more priests or more fallen women. Take off some clothes. Make your characters sweat. Put them in a box. What you want is a hurtling, mad, desperate sense of things falling apart. Have you brought the cops in yet? Has anyone broken a bone? Have all the pies been thrown?

In the best sketch comedy, limits get pushed to the point of raving madness, full psychic deconstruction for one or more of the characters involved. Exaggeration is your best friend here, and logic should be ignored as much as possible. Be bold and outrageous and your scene will sprout wings and fly. Stick to the typical and your scene will die of ennui.

7. Seek an Emotional Peak

If all is going according to plan now, if your sketch is moving more and more toward the characters' emotional cores, if the stakes are being raised, then a clear emotional peak should naturally emerge from the ruin you've created. This is why it's so important to start with strong comic opposites and real conflict in a closed situation. These are the pressure-cooker elements that will cause the thing to explode. Sketch comedy works best when it goes ballistic. For this to happen, you have to create trouble, increase trouble, compress trouble, and push, push, push.

8. Find a Winner

Who wins? Who loses? To make your sketch comedy truly satisfying to the reader or viewer, you have to achieve some sense of completion or closure. It doesn't matter who ultimately pulls out the (metaphorical) gun and blows his enemy away, but until that gun is drawn and fired, until the body hits the floor, your work is not yet done.

A typical comic sketch might be built on an obnoxious talk-show host who attacks and humiliates his guest. In the end, the host might reduce the guest to a quivering mess, or the guest might throw a fatal choke-hold on the host. Or they could conceivably wind up best of friends. One of four outcomes is possible: Somebody wins or somebody loses or everybody wins or everybody loses. It doesn't matter how the story ends so long as it *does* end. You know a sketch is in trouble when there's nothing to do but fade out and cue the "applause" sign.

9. Change the Frame of Reference

This is where you put a twist or a spin on your sketch to cap the action. Whatever reality you've created, try to find a way to pull back from that reality and show it to be a fantasy of some kind or another. If you have a married couple fighting all the way to a party, pull back from that fight and reveal it to be taking place not on the open road but at a car dealership, where the couple is testing a new car to see if it can sustain the sort of fights they like to have. Changing the frame explosively releases all the tension stored in the sketch. It's the coda, the grace note, and it is not to be ignored. At the very least, it's a useful way to get out of a sketch that otherwise presents no natural out.

In writing sketch comedy, there's a huge temptation just to plunge in, start writing dialogue, and see where the darn thing leads. That's one way of doing it, but I think the whole job is easier and more productive if you work out a *beat outline* before you go to script. A "beat" is a single piece of action or conflict, like, "Bob and Ethyl argue about a book." A beat outline describes, in present-tense prose, all the actions and conflicts of a scene or script. A beat outline for the sketch mentioned above might look something like this:

> I. A couple is sitting in a car. He's a mouse and she's a shrew. They argue over how to get to a party.
>
> II. She starts to complain that he never stops to ask for directions. He counters that she's always nagging him. If she'd just leave him alone, he could concentrate and they'd be there already.
>
> III. She reveals that she didn't want to go to the party in the first place since it's just his boring friends. He says it's better than her boring family.
>
> IV. Now they start to fight in earnest, and the fight turns personal: her bad habits, his receding hairline, her weight, the men she could have married instead of him, etc.
>
> V. One of them has had enough and demands a divorce. The other agrees. They lapse into stony silence, resigned to the dissolution of their marriage.
>
> VI. There's a knock on the car window. It's a car salesman asking them how they like the car. They say that it suits them fine. As they get out of the car and start signing purchase papers, we fade on out.

You can see, I hope, that writing the sketch from a structure like this is a good deal simpler and more reliable than the "hunt 'n' hope" method. As always, it's easier to fix the broken parts of the structure in outline than in script.

There's a variation on sketch-comedy structure in which the force of comic opposition is not present but only implied. Typically, this will be a parody sketch, and the force of opposition is the person or thing or institution being parodied. When Chevy Chase impersonated Gerald Ford on *Saturday Night Live*, Ford was the implied force of opposition. Likewise, when Dana Carvey and Mike Meyers did *Wayne's World*, they were mocking, and had implicit conflict with, the whole phenomenon of self-indulgent public-access cable-television shows.

The danger of this structure is that a great comic idea can go flat fast if it doesn't have a strong story and real conflict to keep it moving forward. It's not enough for the Church Lady to parody sanctimony—she has to have a true target, an enemy, nothing less than . . . SATAN!!! against which to vent her spleen.

The best sketch comedy creates characters who slip into the public consciousness and become old friends. The Church Lady, Wayne and Garth, Edith Ann all became pop-cultural icons, so that the just showing the character again was enough to get a laugh again. These characters can become franchises for their creators. If you want such a franchise, start with strong comic characters. If you're lucky, one will break through, and the vast revenue stream of T-shirt licensing will flow for you.

Here's an outline for a comic sketch.

> A self-styled expert is being interviewed on TV. We know he's the comic character when it becomes clear that this self-styled expert knows nothing about his field. The interviewer is his force of opposition, someone determined to expose the fraud. The union is forced by the set-glue of the television show. The conflict escalates as the interviewer challenges the "expert's" expertise. The stakes get raised when the expert's ignorance proves potentially menacing or even deadly for those who follow his advice. The limits get pushed when the expert can no longer ignore the evidence that he's a fraud. An emotional peak gets reached when the expert suffers nervous collapse at the realization of the damage he's done. The winner is the interviewer, who has cut the so-called expert down to size.

The frame gets changed when we discover that the interviewer and the expert are brothers, and this war is really over which of them was mother's favorite son.

Here's another example of escalation in a comic sketch, this one from Monty Python:

A man walks into a waiting room and a mirror falls off the wall. He tries to set it right and a book case falls over. A maid comes in to clean up and the man accidentally stabs her to death. Someone comes to investigate and inadvertently plummets out a window. Policemen come to arrest our hero and all have heart attacks and die. The man leaves the waiting room as objects shatter and walls collapse in his wake. Finally, he steps outside and the whole building explodes.

The man in the waiting room is the comic character. His comic perspective is, "Accidents happen to me." His force of opposition is the magical power at work in that room. His forced union is the need to wait for his appointment. Escalation happens in a line from the mirror to the bookcase to the maid. The stakes get raised when he's arrested for murder. His emotional peak is the realization that destruction is all around him and unavoidable. He wins by escaping, and the frame is changed—literally—when the building ceases to exist.

Another way to look at sketch comedy is to think in terms of creating and then destroying reality. The very act of bringing a reader or a viewer into a scene raises the question, "What's supposed to be funny here?" or, to put it another way, "What's wrong with this picture?" The question creates tension, and when you destroy the scene's reality, you release that tension in laughter.

A kid goes to a gas station to inflate a basketball. As he wrestles with the air hose, the attendant solemnly informs him that hose only pumps "tire air"; it won't work in a basketball at all. The attendant is the comic character, the kid is his foil, and the gas-station setting is their forced union. Tension is created by the question, "Is this guy on the level?" He escalates the conflict through increasingly persuasive arguments that tire air won't work in basketballs. The stakes get raised when a crowd gathers and takes sides on the question. The limit is pushed—and reality is destroyed—when the attendant ultimately fills that ball so full of air that it explodes in the kid's hands. "See, kid? I told you this air wouldn't work." The attendant wins and the kid loses. Finally, we change the frame by revealing that this is a documentary training film on "How to spot morons in the workplace."

Try this exercise: Pretend you're a writer on *Saturday Night Live.* Create a sketch character who can become a pop icon. Put him or her in a repeatable situation and create a strong force of opposition. Now put them in motion. Write a sketch around the forced union of these incompatibles, escalate their stakes, move toward victory for someone, and then wait for the T-shirt royalties to start rolling in.

Sketch comedy seems like a place where you can just dive in and swim around and see what you find. Well, yeah, you can, but without planning, structure, and a sense of destination, your sketch is doomed to dissipate its own energy, wasting whatever terrific comic idea you might have had in the first place. You've seen this happen a thousand times on television and stage. The heartbreak of bad sketch comedy: Don't let it happen to you.

14
TOWARD POLISH AND PERFECTION

Kill your ferocious editor! Procrastinate later! Eradicate fear! Don't judge! Concentrate on process, not product! And quantity, not quality! Get those words on the page! Avoid value judgments! Value judgments are bad! Just do it!

There, I've used up my quota of exclamation points for the year to remind you once again that the death of your ferocious editor is a consummation devoutly to be wished. Now, having helped you kill your ferocious editor, I want to help you rebuild the beast, for finally he has a useful role to play.

We suspend value judgments and lower expectations because we want our creativity to flow. But once the raw material is assembled on the page, we have to make of it something finished and polished and wonderful. This requires not just a ferocious editor but a hard-eyed and relentless one with nerves of steel and an unflagging commitment to quality. If you want to take your material to the next level, nothing less will do.

This will engage your ego. It has to. We all fall in love with our work or our words. This joke or sketch or script or comic opera, it's your baby, and everyone thinks their baby is the cutest in the world. And you're right; your baby *is* cute.

But not as cute as it's going to be.

The goal here is to make your work clever and smooth and funny and elegant and just generally unfailingly admirable in every way. How do you achieve that goal? By rewriting and refining your words. By questioning and rethinking every creative decision you've made up till now. By fine-tuning everything. By going all the way back to square one, if necessary, in pursuit of comic excellence.

Let's not kid ourselves, this is a lot of hard work. Ego questions aside, there's a huge temptation to say that good enough is good enough and move on to the next project. In general, we all want to be done as quickly as possible.

But the hard truth is that the real work of comic writing takes place in rewriting. This is where the jokes become three-dimensional, where characters become true and consistent and emotionally resonant, and where stories shake out their problems and start to take on a compelling life of their own. If you're not willing to commit to rewriting and editing, you might as well go drive a truck.

You will go through hell in rewriting. You will look at a joke and say, "Hell, it's fine just the way it is." You'll look at a plot hole and say, "Maybe nobody will notice." You'll look at story problems and say, "I can't fix them, so I might as well ignore them and hope they go away." For every desire you have to improve the work, there will be an equal and opposite desire to protect your ego instead. This creates a dynamic conflict within, and it can make you very unhappy. Eventually you have to decide whom to serve.

Will you serve your ego, or will you serve your work?

The line of least resistance is to serve the ego. You risk less and you stay comparatively safe. But the real path to success in comic writing lies in serving the work. Insofar as possible, you have to set your ego aside. Here are a few strategies that I find useful when, having clubbed my ferocious editor like a seal pup, I now find that I must somehow bring him back to full and vibrant and productive life.

MINING AND REFINING

You don't dig a gold necklace out of the ground. First you mine the ore, grinding down a ton of gravel to produce an ounce of gold. Next you refine it, smelting and polishing and working the gold until its quality comes through. Using this model, you can see in an instant that it's unrealistic to expect your raw material and your finished product to be one and the same.

And yet we cling to the belief that our raw drafts and first passes are different somehow from humble gold ore. We want it to be that our first effort is our best effort. It saves time and effort, plus wear and tear on the ego. Once you see comic writing as a process of mining and refining, though, you give yourself a way to step past this roadblock and into the world of rewriting, where the true beauty of your work can shine.

Mining your work means pouring everything out on the page where you can look at it, mold it, study it, move the pieces around, whip it into shape. Refining the work means rewriting small and large pieces, changing a word here, a sentence there, a chapter over somewhere around the corner. Once again, we break our process down into separate steps. Concentrate on mining when you're mining, then concentrate on refining when you're refining. The mere act of separating these functions gives a big kick in the quality to both.

As it happens, our minds process information in many different ways. In creative terms, this means that we can go only so far with material we only think about. To get the most out of your comic efforts, you have to put the words or drawings on the page where you can study them, reflect upon them, and bring them up to the next level.

Remember, it's far, far easier to turn bad material into good material, or good material into great material, than it is to get everything (or even *anything*) right on the first try. Break it down. Mine it, then refine it.

Go back now and rewrite any (or every) earlier exercise in this book. I promise that your work will be better for the effort.

WRITE FAST, WRITE LONG

It's easier to cut bad material out than to put new material in. As a function of mining and refining, write everything you can think of now, and sort out later what's relevant and what's not. I'm using this tool even as we speak, writing a small discourse on how I'm using this tool even as we speak. I may decide later that this passage is irrelevant. I may decide it's redundant. I may cut it in the mid—

If you're writing a 120-page script, think about letting your first pass run 160, 170 pages or more. If you need five minutes of stand-up material, write fifteen. If you need to fill one newspaper column with copy, write two or three. If you're doing a comic strips, draw five or six times as many as you need, just to give yourself somewhere to fall.

At every opportunity, present yourself with the *challenge to cut*. Why is this a good idea? Because if you force yourself to cut, say, 50% of your existing work, the 50% that remains will have withstood a fairly rigorous test. By natural selection, the strongest material is always left standing. Write long and cut relentlessly, to the benefit of your work.

When you write long, you can make refining a painless process. Why? Because if you know that the work is a third too long, then you know that you won't be done until all that excess material is excised. This makes the edited work a *happy ending*, the realization of a goal, rather than the death, word-by-painful-word, of some close and cherished friends.

Additionally, when you write long and then cut hard, you find that the work naturally tightens up, becomes sleeker and smoother. If you've met the challenge of cutting down a vastly overwritten document, what's left has to be better than what you had going in. *Has* to be.

Just for drill, write a one-page description of a comic character, and then edit it down to half that length. Far from losing meaning and nuance, your half-page description will be all ways a better read than your first pass was.

GOOD IS THE ENEMY OF THE GREAT

A lot of times when I'm rewriting, I'm confronted with the challenge of cutting material I like. Maybe there's a joke that I really love, but it's not relevant to my story. Maybe I realize that a character I'm really quite fond of needs to be rebuilt from scratch. Maybe I see story problems in an otherwise zippy and satisfying scene. Sometimes I have to go all the way back and rewrite my story before I push on with the script. All of these revelations amount to the same thing: To move forward from this point, I'm going to have to *give up some gains*. There are two strong disincentives for doing so. The first, of course, is that giving up my gains means more work for me, and generally I'm in favor of *less* work for me, not more. Second, giving up my gains is a challenge to my ego. Why wasn't it right the first time, I wonder, and then I feel bad. Can you see my lip pout?

One strategy for getting over this hurdle is something called *the hill-climbing problem.*

Imagine you're standing on top of a fairly high hill. It's an okay place to be, but not the best place in the world. From where you stand, you can see the top of a mountain. *That,* that's where you really want to be. How do you get there?

By going down the hill, of course.

Trouble is, there's a valley between the hill and the mountain, and that valley is filled with fog. I can see the path leading down off the hill, but I can't see any sure way through the fog and up the mountain. In other words, I know what I have to lose (the joke, the character, the time I've invested so far), but I don't know for sure if the sacrifice will ever pay off.

That's the trouble with rewriting. You have to commit to sacrifice with no certain expectation of reward. Yet even absent that guarantee, there's one thing we know for sure: If we don't come down off the hill, we'll never reach the mountain.

In the end, we're faced with a choice between "maybe don't succeed" and "surely don't succeed." When you put the choice in those terms, it's easy to commit to coming down off that hill.

Here's something that makes it easier still.

When we write a joke or a scene or a story, we're reluctant to let any of it go, because we're never altogether sure that we can replace it with something better. We're informed by the fear that *the last idea we had is the last good idea we'll ever have.* This fear makes us hold onto a mediocre joke or essay or cartoon or script or performance or sketch. Even when we *know for certain* that the work's not as good as it could be, we fear that it's already as good as we can make it. If we happened to be right about that, then committing to rewriting any of it would be condemning ourselves to failure, to ego death, and to full-on creative core meltdown.

But I'm convinced that the myth of the last great idea is just that—a myth. Let me see if I can sell you, too.

Suppose you wrote a joke, a pretty darn good one, but one

that you felt could be better still. The myth of the last great idea will tell you to leave well enough alone. But consider this: When you first wrote the joke, you didn't have *that very joke* to draw upon as a resource. If you commit to searching for something better, you'll bring to the task more experience (specifically, the experience of writing the only-okay joke) than you had when you started out. You have to be more successful because you've lived with the material longer, you're more practiced and experienced than you were before.

Now extrapolate this thinking to encompass a whole script or novel or work of comic non-fiction. Taking this work to the next level is now a function of drawing on the work *at this level.* You have more raw material to draw on, more substance to mine and refine; the work can't help but improve.

If you haven't experienced this in your creative work, take the time to prove it to yourself now. Go back and find a joke or comic notion or anything else that you've created in the course of reading this book. In fact, search for the work you like best of all. Now rewrite it. It's unconditionally guaranteed to improve. Try it and see.

The hill-climbing problem and the myth of the last great idea both resonate of the following Zennish phrase: *Good is the enemy of the great.* As long as you're willing to stay comfortable, as long as you'll settle for something that sort of works, you have no hope of achieving real excellence. The myth of the last great idea helps you to rationalize standing pat, but the hill-climbing problem drags you down the hill and into the fog. You may not reach the mountain, but at least you won't be stuck on the hill.

Interestingly, this whole change-is-growth strategy pays dividends in other parts of your life besides writing. We get comfortable. We get stuck in our habits, settled in our ways. Above all, we become reluctant to try for something better for fear of running into something worse. What I've tried to show in this section is that there's always improvement to be had, and that the improvement is grounded in, and aided by, the very set of experiences that seem to need improvement. This takes us right back to process-not-product. Moving forward is moving forward, no matter which direction you choose.

TRUST YOURSELF

Still, all other things being equal, we like to move in the right direction, not the wrong one. How do you know if what you've written is truly funny or only seemingly funny? In the end, you have to trust yourself, your vision, your judgment. But you want to make sure that that judgment is trustworthy. To validate your "yes," you have to authenticate your "no."

At every turn we ask ourselves the question, "Is that line good enough? Is my work done here? Can I move on?" If you have long experience of saying, "No, that doesn't work," and going back and rewriting, then you'll be able to believe it when you finally say, "Yes, *now* it works."

Evaluate your work with your eyes wide open. Since you didn't expect to get it right on the first try, it shouldn't be all that painful to admit that it's not right yet. And if you can view your own work as flawed and imperfect, and survive that harsh self-judgment, then you'll be able to trust the moment when you feel, beyond doubt, that you've taken your work into the rarefied air of excellence.

Avoid falling in love with your jokes. Even though it's funny, who says it can't be funnier still? Avoid closure; the longer you put off saying you're done, the better your finish will be.

Okay, that's perfect for a perfect world, but this isn't one. There are times when you can't trust yourself. Who can you trust instead?

YOUR BETA TESTERS

We get too close to our work. We fall in love with our jokes. We ignore plotholes. We overlook errors. We laugh at jokoids. We imagine that we've achieved perfection when all we've achieved is confusion. Before we force our work on an unsuspecting public, it's useful to force it on a few unsuspecting friends or loved ones first. We call these people our *beta testers*.

The term "beta tester" comes from computer software development. Beta testers are people outside a company who "test drive" new software and report any program bugs or problems back to the developer. This is exactly what your beta testers do for you. They tell you what's right and wrong with your work before you expose it to the world at large.

You probably won't want to use a beta tester. Your ego will engage, and fear will keep you from exposing your work to anyone, especially someone you like. Once again, then, you'll have to decide whether you intend to serve your ego or serve the work. If the latter, then beta testing is vital. No matter how good you are at editing your own work, your perspective is limited. You need someone else to tell you where you've strayed from your story, or missed your joke, or just gone weird.

Beta testers aren't all bad news. Part of their job is to tell you what works in your material and why. The main part of their job is to tell you how to make your good work better. A good beta tester is worth his weight in jokes.

Is one beta tester enough? Yes, if he or she is smart and honest and clear-eyed and hard-working. More is better, because no one beta tester will see everything there is to see in your work. Eventually you'll reach a point of diminishing returns, though; just as too many cooks pop the soufflé, too many beta testers will just confuse and contradict and dismay.

Finding Beta Testers

Who makes a good beta tester? A husband or wife? Parents? Friends? Paid professionals? These are all options, but all have their drawbacks. Paid readers, for instance, may be knowledgeable but cost too much. Your mother will be far more likely to feed your ego than to improve the work. Spouses or lovers make excellent beta testers because they're already part of your life and (presumably) supportive of your creative goals. On the other hand, the relationship between writer and tester can be a tumultuous one; friendships, even love affairs, have been known to die in that fire.

Must your beta tester be an expert in your comic genre? No, but it helps. If you're writing stand-up comedy, for example, you want your beta tester to be at least a fan of stand-up so that he or she can make informed, useful comments on your work. You don't want a beta tester who says only, "I liked it," or, "This didn't work for me," or even, "Are you out of your freaking mind?" Your beta tester should be able to articulate full and concrete responses to your work.

On the other hand, you want a beta tester who can read you without prejudice. That is, you don't want a tester who's a potential employer or client or buyer of your work. Beta testers see raw material and rough drafts. Show this unpolished material to a highly placed person in your field and you risk queering that person's opinion of you and your work. You want to save these valuable contacts for later, when you've sharpened your material to a rapier point and you're ready to blow them away with your brilliance.

Peers make your best beta testers. Find people working at about your level and within your area of interest. Be willing to return the favor and beta test for them. This not only puts them in your debt, but also gives you a chance to learn from someone else's mistakes besides your own. Look for beta testers among fellow students in classes you take, or seminars you attend, or dive bars where you hang out. Try to find people who share your sensibility and your sense of humor, but don't get too hung up on that. The most important quality for a beta tester is a willingness to help.

Training Your Beta Tester

The last thing you want is someone who loves every word you write, or every joke you tell, or every cartoon you draw. The point of using a beta tester is to improve your work, and how can you improve on something that someone loves unconditionally? Then again, you don't want your beta tester to tell you he hated your work unless he can tell you why. The ideal beta tester gives detailed notes on your work, tells you specifically what he did or didn't like, and why. People like these are made, not born.

So tell your beta tester what you're looking for: not a pat on the back nor a blanket rebuke, but a clear path to improving your work. Give him as much information as possible about what you're trying to accomplish so that he can tell you whether you've done it or not.

Train your beta tester to think in terms of *large notes* and *small notes*. Large notes are general comments about the structure and theme of your work, about your story and characters. Small notes are line notes: This joke works, that scene direction is unclear, this paragraph seems redundant, etc.

Also train your beta tester to be honest. He won't necessarily want to be honest, especially if he thinks he'll hurt your feelings. Tell him you don't want a cheerleader; that's what mom is for. The key phrase here is *constructive criticism*. Explain to your beta tester that all news is good news if it helps improve your work. If you can demonstrate to your beta tester that you're serving the work and not the ego, he is likely to do the same.

Recognize that a relationship with your beta tester is a long-term one. Just as you don't master tools on the first try, your beta tester won't give you at first the sort of useful, detailed critique that you'll get later on. This is one reason why it's better to train a friend or a lover or a peer to be a beta tester than it is to hire someone to do the job. Teach a man to fish and you feed him for life.

Let your beta tester know which of his comments you find most useful and why. Seek *detail* at every turn. It's useful to know, for example, which lines made your beta tester laugh so that you can study those lines and write more like them. It's also useful for your beta tester to tell you where he got confused or unamused or just plain lost interest. The more clearly you can tell your beta tester how he's being helpful, the more helpful he can be in return.

Using Your Beta Tester

Using your beta tester is really about training yourself how to accept his notes. This isn't easy. When your beta tester tells you that he doesn't get a joke, and it happens to be your favorite joke, you'll be inclined to tell your beta tester, "Well, then you must be stupid," or words to that effect.

You can see how this might not be the best thing for a working relationship.

I try to say as little as possible when my beta tester is giving me notes. I'm not there to argue or defend or explain; I'm only there to listen. There's no point in asking for an opinion if you're not going to listen to it.

You don't have to agree with everything your beta tester says. You don't have to agree with *anything* your beta tester says. No matter how well-considered his opinion is, it's still just an opinion. You are the creator, which means in at least one sense that you are God. God may take advice from cherubim and angels, but in the end what God says goes.

So don't rewrite to please your beta tester. This isn't always easy to do. Since your beta tester is your first audience, and you want to please the audience, you run the risk of following his vision rather than your own. Resist this temptation, for you'll only end up trying to serve two masters, to the detriment of the work. Adopt those suggestions you find useful and set aside (after careful consideration) those that you decline to use. Make it clear to your beta tester that you haven't ignored his notes; above all, treat him with respect, for his is a truly thankless job.

If a beta tester rejects a joke, take it as a challenge. Even though you love the joke, replace it with something else, just to prove to yourself that it can be done. Even if you think the joke works—*especially* if you think it works—seize the opportunity of making it better still.

What follows now may be the toughest exercise in this whole book: Take something you've written recently, give it to someone, and ask them to give you detailed notes. Then rewrite the piece from those notes. For the purposes of this exercise, assume that *everything* your beta tester tells you is dead-on useful and correct.

HOW DONE IS DONE?

How do you know when you've taken your comic masterpiece as far as it can go? I wish I could give you a tool for this, but I can't. I can only tell you from my own experience that sooner or later I always "hit the wall" with my projects. Sooner or later I know that I've rewritten and tested and rewritten and tested and rewritten the work to the best of my good faith and ability. I reach a point of diminishing return. Past that point, no matter how long I continue to noodle with the work, it's just that: noodling.

I also always know when I haven't hit the wall, when I haven't pushed myself as hard as I can. I think we all know when we're cheating the process, but ego and inertia keep us from admitting this to ourselves. When you push yourself to the limit, you not only improve the work, but you also improve your awareness of what your limit is. To put it another way, if you push your limits, they become less limiting.

Winston Churchill said,

> *Writing a book is an adventure. To begin with, it is a toy and an amusement. Then it becomes a mistress, then it becomes a master, then it becomes a tyrant. The last phase is that just as you are about to become reconciled to your servitude, you kill the monster and fling him to the public.*

This chapter, for instance. I think I've flogged it long enough, and that I shall kill it now and fling it to the public. My beta testers, of course, may disagree . . .

15

SCRAPMETAL AND DOUGHNUTS

Fresh out of college, armed with a virtually worthless degree in creative writing, aspiring to no loftier goal than making the world safe for advertising, I interviewed for a job as a copywriter. To say that the pay was meager makes meager look good, but I was eager to prove my corporate mettle, so I solemnly declared my willingness to work, as I put it then, "for scrapmetal and doughnuts." I don't know what impressed them more, my elegant turn of the phrase, or my naked lust for indentured servitude. In any case, I got the job, went on to a meteoric eighteen months in the ad biz, named three automatic teller machines, wrote a recruitment campaign for flight attendants, crashed and burned in spectacular fashion, and moved on to the challenge of unemployment.

But that phrase "scrapmetal and doughnuts" has always stayed in my mind, and it's always stood in my mind for the leftovers, the corners of things, that which is overlooked. Here, then, are the scrapmetal and doughnuts of the comic toolbox, stuff that I couldn't find a place for elsewhere and didn't want to leave for the sequel.

THE WINCE FACTOR

A songwriter friend of mine always used this trick to check out the lyrics of her songs. She'd sing them to herself and listen for the words that made her wince. She figured that if they made her wince, they'd probably have the same effect on others. She used the wince factor to edit her work. I do the same, and so can you. This has less to do with how to be funny than with how not to be not-funny.

When you're reading your work for quality and style, pay attention to your own wince factor. If you're clear-eyed and honest in your appraisal of your own work, you'll know when a joke is flat or a line goes clang. Be rigorous. Don't let yourself off the hook. If you're at all uncertain about whether something works, spend some time and skull sweat, and wipe that uncertainty away.

The thing about the wince factor is that you can use it to turn a bad thing into a good thing. Learn to take pride in your ability to ferret out the winces, chase them away, and change them into lines you like. You could even keep score.

Above all, remember this: It's far better for the line to make you wince now than to make someone else wince later. Police your prose.

And speaking of police, let me introduce you to

THE FRAUD POLICE

The first time I ever taught a class, I found myself standing before a large group of students who expected me to be funny, witty, entertaining, knowledgeable, and intelligent. Because I feared I was not these things, a huge amount of tension built up within me, like the electrostatic charge in a Van de Graaff generator. That tension was obvious to everyone and made the entire class feel uncomfortable. This, of course, made me more uncomfortable, which in turn made them more uncomfortable, which made me more uncomfortable still, and so on and so forth until we were all a bunch of frantic Chicken Littles, sitting around waiting for the sky to fall.

I had this deep, primal fear that someone would discover that I had no business teaching the class I'd been hired to teach, like those dreams where you show up naked and unprepared for final exams in high school. I also had a hunch that as long as I tried to hide my fear, it would haunt me, degrade my performance, and possibly ruin the class. So I copped to the fear. I told my students that this was my first time teaching, that I was swimming in strange waters, and, in fact, expected the fraud police to kick down the door any moment and haul me away to phony-teacher's prison.

Well, you know by now that I was telling a lie to comic effect, using exaggeration and detail to make the gag bigger and clearer, and releasing the stored collective tension. I got a laugh, but more to the point, I stumbled on a truth and pain common to creative people: We all fear the fraud police. Why? Because creative people naturally seek challenges larger and more daunting than ones they've mastered before. This means we're *always* swimming in strange waters. Which means that the fraud police are never far away.

But here again, giving a thing a label helps us deal with it constructively. Just as we invoke the wince factor to attack bad writing, we summon the fraud police to unmask our fears. Once you tell people what you're afraid of, you no longer have to worry about their finding that thing out. They already know. And since they're most likely afraid of the very same stuff, they sympathize and empathize. You become their hero.

Any time you're in a new situation, fear is present. It has to be, based on the newness of the situation alone. If you deny or repress that fear, then it becomes hidden tension. It increases your anxiety and degrades your performance. But as soon as you admit your fear, the tension goes away, anxiety lessens, and performance improves.

Suppose you're doing stand-up comedy for the first time. Suppose the audience knows it's your first time. They're aware that you might bomb horribly and that they might have to serve embarrassed witness to the unsightly mess you make. They feel tense. Relieve that tension and they'll be your friends for life. Say these words: "Be gentle with me, it's my first time." The audience will laugh at the clash of context, but more important, they'll be grateful to you for acknowledging the fraud police. You've taken them off the hook. They no longer have to judge; now they can just enjoy.

It's a situational oxymoron: To divert the fraud police, invite them into your home. If you reveal your secret, no one can find it out. This is wildly liberating, both to you and to your audience.

Finally, recognize your own inner fraud police. Think of them as the goon squad of your ferocious editor, always willing to judge and condemn, judge and condemn, to haul you off to a small room someplace where bad things happen. They tell you in secret, silent voices that you have no business doing the very thing you want most in the world to do. They're trying to get you to admit that you're unworthy. But if you already *know* that you're unworthy, then they lose all their power over you. Launch a pre-emptive strike on the fraud police and the fuzz becomes your friend.

CHARACTER KEYS

Character keys are the small ways a character behaves that tell us the large ways he'll behave as well. Think of a character key as the intersection of microconflict and comic perspective. Character keys are useful ways to introduce characters to a reader or an audience at the beginning of a story or a script. At their best, they tell us in an instant what we can expect from a given comic character in almost every situation.

If, for example, we have a character whose strong comic perspective is *innocence*, then we might meet her in a moment when she opens her mail, reads a letter from Publisher's Clearinghouse, turns to her husband, and cries excitedly, "Look, honey! Ed McMahon says I may already have won!" Through this character key, this small, revealing action, we know this character instantly to be naive, unworldly, borderline stupid. It will not surprise us, then, to find this naiveté informing all of her actions.

In *Tootsie*, we first meet the character of Sandy at Michael Dorsey's birthday party. She concludes her birthday toast with, "I'm sorry, this is a really stupid speech." In this moment, we know Sandy to be neurotic and insecure. We have a line on her. In the same scene, Michael's roommate, Jeff, solemnly declares that he doesn't want people to like his plays. He wants people to say, "I saw your play, man. What *happened*?" His *auteur* pose is instantly, permanently, and crystally clear.

To build audience allegiance early in your story or script, lay in precise and powerful character keys that give readers or viewers an immediate grasp of your characters' attitudes and attributes. You might say that I did this on the very first page of the book, introducing myself as someone who *blurts things out*. Isn't this true? Aren't I still blurting? Have I not blurted all along?

A character key is a small, defining action. As an exercise, pick a character you've previously created and describe in a sentence some action that will make his strong comic perspective vivid and clear to us. Oh heck, do a couple.

FRAMES OF REFERENCE

Comedy is a popular art form. To succeed in comedy, you have to be popular. That means that your humor has to work for a broad audience, or at least for its intended audience. In assimilating your audience's frame of reference, there are two things to be aware of: what your audience knows and what your audience accepts.

We've already talked about knowing what your audience knows and about the difference between the class clown and the class nerd. But what your audience knows is a dynamic thing. It's constantly changing. New information becomes available, and old information becomes tired and fades away. Today's hot topic is tomorrow's yesterday's news.

On the other hand, if the topic of your humor is so hot and new that your audience hasn't heard of it yet, you'll be left all alone way out ahead of the curve. Talk about the latest findings in *The New England Journal of Medicine* and you'll likely face blank stares at best, empty seats at worst. You have to strike a balance.

How can you know your audience's current frame of reference? You can't, not always and never absolutely. The best you can do is guess and conjecture, and above all test. Test your material with as many people as possible and find out what they find funny and what they don't. Be prepared to change your material, either in structure or in substance, in order to hit your target. Here's another strong argument for not falling in love with your jokes: If you do, you'll go on telling the same jokes long after they've stopped being funny.

Also, be aware that I'm not speaking only of stand-up comics and live audiences here. If you're writing comedy on the page, or drawing cartoons, you have to be that much more rigorous in assuring that your material won't fade. Go for the cheap topical reference and you're only planting the seeds of your own destruction. Great Flood of '93. See what I mean?

What will an audience accept? This gets into questions of taste and taboos, propriety and political correctness. For example, do you remember when drugs were funny? In the early 1980s, you couldn't swing a dead cat without hitting a TV sitcom episode about cocaine or marijuana. Hilarious stuff. By the early 1990s, drugs were passé, and anyone pitching drug humor in a network sitcom story meeting was asking for a quick ticket to the parking lot.

Things change. Tastes change. You have to change with the times.

Does this mean you should seek not to offend? Of course not. Your humor is your humor, and one man's offense is another man's boffo gag. It's okay to offend *part* of your audience if you connect with another part. If you offend too many and amuse too few, though, you'll have no audience at all. And humor requires an audience.

It's okay if some people really hate your stuff. That means they feel strongly about it, and this admits the possibility that others will love it just as strongly. The place you want to avoid is the vast, bland middle ground where your humor is safe, innocuous, offensive to no one—and thus compelling to no one. You want your humor to move people, and that won't happen unless your choices are bold.

So don't be afraid to offend. In fact, you can turn offense to your advantage. Consider the stand-up comic who attacks and insults a heckler. Sure, he offends the heckler, but in so doing he creates a strong bond between himself and the rest of the audience. It's an "us versus him" mentality, what we might call the Saddam Hussein effect: The best way to unify a people is to give them a common enemy. That heckler is the audience's common enemy, and the comic who attacks the heckler can be as brutal as he wants *to the heckler* without losing his audience.

You might write a comic essay attacking, oh, say, insurance salesmen. You can say what you like about insurance salesmen (*"As if life insurance worked . . ."*) because your audience is not insurance salesmen, but rather the hapless victims of same. You and your audience are unified against the common enemy. They'll accept anything you dish out.

Just don't try publishing that essay in *Insurance Salesmen's Quarterly.*

As an exercise, pick something or someone that really, really bugs you—taxes, family, bad driving, how-to books—and attack it in the form of a comic essay. Be as brutal and offensive as possible. But be careful who you show it to. I wouldn't want you to get hurt.

In the end, of course, you have to please yourself. So always make sure that your humor delights that most important audience of one. If you genuinely find your stuff funny, chances are that a certain fixed percentage of the rest of the world will, too. And hey, if they don't like it, the worst they can do is ignore you. Or possibly hang you. Really, what've you got to lose?

YOUR COMIC VOCABULARY

Not every joke you think of is useful to you now. A lot of good jokes get scrapped in the service of a stronger story. Many comic notions show great promise but can't stand the weight of development. Sometimes you're just ahead of an audience's understanding. In the course of your career, you'll collect quite a lot of this comic flotsam. Start saving it now. Consider it to be the great tinfoil ball of your life. Anything becomes valuable if you hold onto it long enough.

I have a file labeled "1001 Clever Things I Thought Up Myself or Stole From a Few Close, Personal Friends." Into this file goes funny stuff for which I can find no current use: jokes written on napkins ("Coffee is better than sex because you can have more coffee right away"), words of wisdom ("The rules don't confine, they *de*fine"), inspirational slogans ("Self-indulgence is its own reward"), oxymorons, funny names, ear tickles, etc. Is this stuff worth saving? At worst, it takes up (minimal) space on my hard disk. At best, it all contributes to a valuable resource called my comic vocabulary.

Items in my comic vocabulary may lie fallow for years before finding new lives and new homes in stories or scripts or stand-up routines or one-panel cartoons. When I'm stuck for an idea or a joke, I go back and review my comic vocabulary. Maybe I'll find something directly useful, or maybe I'll stumble across something that triggers a new idea. Maybe the mere act of reading old jokes (or things I once thought were jokes) will set my mind thinking in productive new ways. My comic vocabulary is both an inventory and a stimulus. So's yours.

Start now to build your comic vocabulary. Get in the habit of writing down the funny things you say or think. Don't worry if they don't look funny on the page, for your comic vocabulary is a very private file that no one else will see (until, perhaps, after you're dead, and then, really, what will you care?). Also don't worry if these bits lack structure or context. After all, if they had structure and context, you'd have used them somewhere else already.

As a discipline, try to add five or ten new jokes or jokoids to the file every day. You'll have a formidable storehouse of collected wit (or half-collected half-wit) a lot sooner than you think.

THE WADE BOGGS PARADIGM

Wade Boggs used to play third base for the Boston Red Sox (and parenthetically, if you want to know about comedy, truth, and pain, try being a Red Sox fan in this lifetime). Wade Boggs had a staggering batting average. He hit over .300 every year and was arguably the best pure hitter in baseball.

And he took batting practice every day. The best pure hitter in baseball felt the need to step into the batting cage every day and do the grunt-work of his craft.

Now look, you and I aren't as good at making comedy as Wade Boggs was at hitting a baseball. Never will be. And yet we don't practice our craft every day. Somehow we've gotten it into our heads that we don't have to. The purpose of the Wade Boggs Paradigm is to remind us that we do. It's like this: If Wade Boggs practices, and he's better than we are, then it stands to reason that we could stand to practice, too.

This is not bad news. Because when we practice our craft, we not only get better at it, we also build up a body of work, stuff we can use to impress our parents, make our friends laugh, possibly even *sell* one day. But this all only happens if we plant our butts in our chairs, or grab that cartooning pen, or stand up there on that cold, dark stage and do it. Wouldn't you like to be as good as Wade Boggs? It's like that old joke about how to get to Carnegie

Hall. "Practice, son, practice."

If you're not the comic creator you want to be, I'm willing to bet that it's not because you aren't funny. Hell, if you genuinely weren't funny, I think you'd know it, and you wouldn't want to be a comic creator in the first place. Nor would you have swapped hard currency for this book. If you're not as funny as you want to be, perhaps you're not *working hard enough*. But rest assured that someone else out there is working hard enough, working twice as hard as you. If you want to be successful, you're going to have to take a lot more batting practice than you ever imagined. And you're never going to stop, not even when you become successful. Because as soon as you stop practicing, your skills begin to fade.

So how do you practice comedy? Easy. If you're a writer, you write. If you're a cartoonist, you draw cartoons. If you're a comic actor, you act comically. If you're a comic photographer, you take funny photographs. No, check that, you take lots and lots and *lots* of photographs and hope and trust that some small number of them will develop into a chuckle or two. Remember, even a .300 hitter makes an out twice as often as he gets a hit. Embrace failure and make practice part of your routine. If it's good enough for Wade Boggs, it's certainly good enough for us.

Oh, and look on the bright side: at least you're not a Red Sox fan. Oh you are? Oh dear . . .

PROBLEM SETS

How do you make a joke? How do you physically, actually, cognitively create a comic moment out of metaphorical thin air? Do you just sit under the apple tree and wait for joke-fruit to bop you on the head? Not unless you've got more time and patience than common sense. Here's a different strategy: Treat the joke as a problem to be solved.

Sometimes this requires nothing more than applying a tool to a situation. You can, for instance, apply clash of context to a ghost town and get a Manhattan nightclub or an aircraft carrier in the middle of the Mojave Desert. You can apply exaggeration to a late-night television commercial and find a line like, "If you act now, we'll include the entire state of Rhode Island at no extra charge!" You can attach a wildly inappropriate response to a high-school pep rally and get the cheerleaders doing a striptease or the band playing a funeral dirge. You can bend a common phrase and discover the difference between an optimist and a pessimist:

> *An optimist looks at the glass and says it's half full.*
> *A pessimist looks at the glass and says, "If I drink*
> *this, I'll probably spill it all over myself and ruin*
> *my shirt."*

Once you get good at this trick, it's like juggling; it's subconscious and automatic. And then you can get even more sophisticated and complex in the construction of your problem sets.

Suppose I want to invent some comic phobias. First I construct the problem set. I find that this set has four parts:

1) What is a trivial or absurd fear?
2) What word for that fear sounds good with the *-phobia* suffix?
3) Is my solution likely to be understood by most readers or viewers or listeners?
4) Does my definition twist or amplify the meaning of the phobia?

Here are some possible solutions to this problem:

Anachrophobia, fear of being out-of-date.
Philatophobia, fear of stamp collectors.
Metaphorophobia, fear of poetic allusions.
Pedestrophobia, fear of walking things.
Prophylactophobia, fear of contraceptive sheaths.
Chihuahuaphobia, fear of yapping small dogs.
Pterydactophobia, fear of flying dinosaurs.
Intoxiphobia, fear of obnoxious drunks.
Bibliophobia, fear of the Dewey Decimal System.
Doughnophobia, fear of fattening breakfast treats.

When I solve for all four parts of the problem set, the joke works, but if I solve for three parts or less, the joke fails. If I say agoraphobia, I'm dealing with a real fear, the fear of crossing open spaces, and not a trivial or absurd one, so that won't work. If I say, "Agraphaphobia, fear of early Christian writings," the word sounds fine but the meaning will be lost on the majority of readers or viewers. If I say, "Angoraphobia, fear of angora sweaters," the fear is trivial, the word sounds fine, the joke is understandable, but the definition doesn't change or amplify the meaning.

Note that you get a little extra bounce out of the joke if it also has an ear tickle, if it sounds like an authentic, pre-existing phobia, as anachrophoba to arachnophobia. But since it's not vital that the joke also tickle the ear, the need for an ear tickle is not part of the problem set.

If this seems way too analytical, well maybe it is. A lot of this process happens automatically, and let's face it, you don't need to know how a watch works in order to tell time. But when you're stuck and you don't know where else to turn for a comic idea, it's useful to have *structure* to fall back on, and thinking of jokes in terms of problems and their solutions is a reliable application of structure.

As an exercise, generate a list of comic "-holics" (scotchoholic, shopoholic, aquaholic, etc.). First, list the terms of your problem set, and then come up with solutions that meet those terms. Then do another exercise where you pose both the problem and the terms of its solution.

The strategy of using problem sets to generate jokes is especially effective when you use the rule of nine and the power of the list, because it's a little mechanical and you don't always get great results. Such is the nature of tools.

LEAPLETS

This is just a pep-rally paragraph, folks. Any time you're frustrated in your ability to use tools, or write jokes, or draw cartoons, or win an audience, or overcome your ego blocks, remember that progress is made in small steps. Creatively, we grow not in leaps but in leaplets. Moving forward slowly is moving forward just the same. Don't expect more of yourself and your tools than they can give you now. Make the best of what you've got and don't drive yourself nuts.

16
HOMILIES AND EXHORTATIONS

I started this book by talking about math class. Throughout the text, I've drawn connections between comedy and arithmetic, comedy and geometry, comedy and quantum mechanics, what-have-you. Now, as we hurtle toward the end, I'd like to introduce one last chunk of pseudo-science, a formula that applies not only to comic writers or artists or performers but to anyone striving to succeed in any field of endeavor. Maybe even in life. Here it is:

TALENT + DRIVE + TIME = SUCCESS

People want to know if they have enough talent to succeed. They seem to think that talent is like S&H Green Stamps—collect enough talent points and you can redeem them for a toaster. Do you have enough talent to succeed? I believe you do. I believe we all do. It's part of our genetic package, like the pancreas or a fear of falling. Talent, the gift of creation, is, in a sense, what separates us from the lichens and squids.

This is not to say that everyone can be a brilliant comedian, any more than everyone can play Brahms with a blindfold or nail a triple pike with a back half-twist at the Olympics. But everyone has talent. It comes with the territory.

So yes, you do have talent. But talent is only one part of the equation. To parlay your talent into success, you have to apply hard work, practice, patience, perseverance, and relentless pursuit of your goals: in sum, drive.

I know many superbly talented writers, for example, who don't get work because they don't have drive. They don't flog themselves to achieve day in and day out, and eventually they just drop out of the race and go sell cars or something. I'd hate like hell to see that happen to you.

So don't ask yourself if you have enough talent; rather, ask if you have enough drive. Do you have the sticktoitiveness to keep pounding away at the word processor or uncapping that drawing pen or dragging yourself up on stage, day after day, week and month after year after decade? If you don't, you might as well go sell cars now because, absent a lightning strike of extraordinary good fortune, you'll never be successful.

That's the bad news. The good news is that you still have time. You have lots and lots of time. Twenty-four hours of it every day. That's an incredibly lot of time in which to get an incredibly lot of work done. While you're still alive and walking around on the planet, you still have time to make your dreams come true. But while it's true that you have more time than you imagine, it's also true that time is your one non-renewable resource. Eventually, alas, time does run out. Time is ours to spend, then, but not to waste.

So here's the math: talent + drive + time; apply sufficient drive to your manifest talent over time and you will succeed. That's my bright promise to you. But there's a catch. You don't just need drive, you need *sufficient* drive.

How much drive is sufficient drive? It's not realistic to expect someone suddenly to turn their lives over to the perfect pursuit of comedy. We all have friends and loved ones, jobs and interests, hobbies and obligations, all of which compete for our time and our attention. Where, then, do we find the energy and motivation to move forward toward our goals? How do we construct a comic creator's life in the context of a busy person's life? It ain't easy. Here's the path I take.

I think of the journey toward my writing goals as a trip down a long road. I can't see the end of the road. I can't be sure there even is an end to the road. And I have no certain expectation of ever arriving there. What, then, do I know for sure? I know that, with every step I take, I'm moving *farther from the beginning*. I may never reach the end of the road, but I can always get farther from the start. Just as I focus on *process, not product*, I also bend my attention to *journey, not destination*. This twist sets me free, for it gives me *success in process* every single day. That fuels my drive, which moves me faster down the road, which increases my measure of success, which further fuels my drive, and so on.

What opposes drive? Fear, mostly. Fear of failure. If you put that manuscript in the mail, you might get rejected. If you go up on stage, you might bomb. If you try to be funny, you might get ignored. Fear is your single strongest disincentive, and though I've tried to give you some strategies for facing fear in this book, in the end that's a battle you have to fight alone. Fight it as aggressively and consciously as possible.

I try to practice patience and impatience simultaneously. I know that there will be days when fear or disincentive or just plain laziness will win out, and on those days I won't get a damn thing done. I can accept those days if I know that yesterday I was productive, and tomorrow (or the next day) I'll be productive again. I take the long view of my career to grant myself patience and the short view of my career to imbue myself with drive. In other words, I try to put myself on the spot and let myself off the hook at the same time.

Creativity, especially comic creativity, is not a constant force. We're never as productive as we want to be or feel we should be, and no matter how much we apply tools to the comic process, there are still powers at work beyond our control. Some days the river runs dry. Those are good days to go to the movies.

Because life is long, and time is plentiful, and because talent is yours by right of birth, you have the means to achieve your dreams—*if* you have the drive. Do you have the drive? There's only one person who can answer that question, and it ain't the guy who wrote this book.

REVELATION

A book can hit a reader with the force of revelation. While you're reading it, and for a short time after, you may feel pumped up, psyched, filled with the sense that anything is possible. Great! Go with that feeling! It's included in the text at no extra charge.

But it will fade, for revelation always fades. Soon you won't have the feeling of enthusiasm but only a *memory* of that feeling, and its hold over you will weaken exponentially. That's the way revelation works: One day you're Paul on the road to Damascus; next day you're just looking at slides from the trip.

I hope you've become excited by some of the tools you found in this book. During the next week, you might use them every day. In the following week, you'll use them less frequently. By week three, four, or five, this book will be just another volume on your bookshelf. This is not sad or lamentable. It's natural, inevitable. Because revelation fades.

But revelation adds huge power to a life. If you're excited and energized about *anything*, it makes you more productive and lends both quality and quantity to your work. So, then, keeping revelation alive is a good thing. But how to achieve that lofty goal? You can't just flip back to page one and start re-reading. Nor can you wait for the sequel, *The Comic Toolbox Two: How to be Funnier than You Already Are*. That book may be a long time in coming.

To keep revelation alive in your life, seek new sources of inspiration. Read books. Take classes. Meditate. Do yoga. Wander in the woods and contemplate the Big Questions. Above all, *create*. Create as much comedy as you can. Don't worry about whether it's any good or whether it will make your wildest dreams come true. The mere act of creation is the strongest, most powerful force of revelation there is. Nothing electrifies a day or an hour or a minute like the act of creation. Make creation a habit in your life. Revelation will flow from this, and success, I do believe, will follow as well.

We struggle with motivation. Mostly we struggle with *self*-motivation. It's easy to be motivated when you have a boss to force your labor. But there's never a boss around when you need one, and providing your own motivation can be tough. I've tried in this book to give you a good swift kick in the motivation and to show you how you can improve your comedy and productivity through logical process and small, small steps. But as I said, revelation fades. What happens next is strictly up to you.

Set new goals. Set aside time to work toward those goals. Recognize that progress comes slowly, and grant yourself the time and the grace to go forward at your own pace. Use your tools to help you get past the "stuck" points and get you moving again.

On the subject of tools, recognize that some of these tools will be more useful to you than others. Some will slip naturally into your comic process while others will feel gawky and awkward. Use the easy ones but don't neglect the troublesome ones. Come back to them later and try again. It may be that you only need to grow a while as a writer or an artist or an actor or a comedian before you can use those difficult tools well. We tend to exercise our stronger muscle groups, but the weak muscles need their workout, too.

Recognize that creativity, especially comic creativity, is a gift. Every time you make someone laugh, you bring joy into the universe and make your world, in some small way, a better place to be. Respect this gift, honor it, and take responsibility for it. Comedy is no innocent thing, but a powerful, often subversive, force for change. It's up to you to decide whether that force will be a positive or a negative one.

I hope you'll make it positive. I hope you'll use your talent and your drive not just to make your life better but to make all life better. I can even tell you why it's in your interest to do so. When you contribute to the common good, you increase the amount of common good floating around out there. The more common good there is, the better are your odds of some of it coming back to you. If that's too goopy for you, consider that working toward positive, humanistic goals brings you into contact with other like-minded people. Aren't these good people the ones you want to know and hang out with and love?

And if nothing else, devoting your vision to positive ends makes you feel better about yourself. If you feel good about yourself, you tend to have good, productive, hard-working, and happy days. Exactly the kind of days you want. In a real sense, when you devote yourself to helping others with your works or words, you improve your ability to bring those words or works to life.

Every creative person has the chance to invest real heart in his or her work. Absent that investment, the best we can hope for is "artoid," the velvet Elvis, not art but an incredible simulation. Art without heart is like, well, like sex without love. Yeah, it's okay, but if you had a choice . . . ?

And you do have a choice. Your comedy can be constructive or destructive. Your art can mock or inform. Your words can degrade or enlighten. What you do is up to you, but if the worst happens and you're *never* the success you want to be, wouldn't you like to be able to look back and say, "At least I did the right thing?" I sure would.

So make your choice and take your stand, and recognize that life is long, fraught with opportunity. Have patience and have fun. You are blessed.